State Prison
MY FIFTEEN YEAR WALK

Sylvester Long
with Julius Justice

UCP
Detroit, Michigan

D1501633

This book is based on actual events, however many of the names have been changed out of respect for those depicted in this book.

Graphic Design (Front Cover) by Dean Bryant
Book Design & Prepress Management by Metri Duley

2007
Published by Urban City Publishing.
www.urbancitypublishing.com
(313) 643-2125

Acknowledgements

Special thanks to God for keeping me strong healthy and sane. To my mother, who stood by me when I was wrong or right and died loving me, with major love. She's my true Angel.

To my family, my three sisters who supported me for fifteen years. And my sister Dee who came to every prison in Michigan to see me and dealt with the ignorance and unfair treatment, just to see me. My cousin Debbie who showed much, much love. My friends Robbin, Toni Dunbar, Angie Cureton, Charlene Chandler and Sharon Graham.

My reason for doing better and wanting something out of life, Kashira and Nesha. Kelena, Lil D, Conya Ada and Man who has my love…

To my cousins Wolf, Vincent, Larry and Andrew, whom I love like brothers and a true friend George.

To my Prison Players; Buckey, Phil, Mike, Hammer, Greg, Calvin, Smith Bey, Melvin Baker, Cee, Lil Walker, Kim Kim, John Murphy, Speedy Butler, Black Dre, Big Ed, Pee Wee Mayhand, Eric Pratt, Dulin Bey, Mr. Will Gill, Mr. Chandler III, Tony Taylor El, Eric Hester, The Fisher Brothers, Donnie B, Shawny, John Walker, Dexter Dre, Spencer Holloway, Ghetti, Kenny G., Fat Cat, Gene, Joe Smelley, Money Green, Player Kwesi, Mr. Joe Watson, Keith, Marcellors Simmons, Orlando Miller, True Player, Steven Williams, Swan-El, Ernie Walton, Fleebag, Boss-Dexter, Big Boss Eastside, D-Smith Battle Creek, Big Sixx, T.Young, Big Porter, Moose, Mike Manning, Player Biz, Young Andy Dexter, Farmer-X, Lo, Herb, Shakey Dre, Arab Nick, Drewpo, and Skibo I Love You…

To Josh and CJ who supported and helped me make this book

possible, Project Rickey, his sister Teresa and Lisa and his mother and father.

All of my homies in State prison, stay up, I will lay the foundation for better living conditions and standards. Even though my mind and body is out here in the so called free world, my heart and soul is still there with the real niggas that helped me grow into a man.

The True King is the King within yourself!!! Life is life as long as you are living, it's a way to do better. Free is a mental concept. They can never lock your mind up. You are always free mentally!!! Move forward my Brothers…

Chapter One

On August 13, 1985 I was found guilty of Second Degree Murder.

At age twenty-five, five feet five inches tall and only one hundred and forty-six pounds, my only thoughts were of the inmates and if I would be tough enough to maintain my manhood. After much worrying though, it would not be the inmates that I would have to worry about, but the corrupt, disrespectful department of corrections staff.

A month after my conviction I was shackled from hand to foot, and taken out of the county jail, chained to seven other men, and marched into a van waiting to take us to Jackson State Prison.

For the next 15 years, prison was about to become my new home. In a matter of hours I would see first hand everything that I had heard about on the streets. However, my primary thoughts at this point was getting my conviction overturned and returning back home to my family. I was convinced that I'd been convicted unfairly on charges that would never stand up on appeal.

As we boarded the bus I looked up at the bright city skies and wondered how long it would be before I saw freedom again. I hoped it would be soon. As we drove through the streets of Detroit, everyone's mood seemed different. Three of the men were talking like it was no big deal. Talking about all the people they knew up in the joint, and all the things they had seen while up there. Stories that quite frankly, I didn't want to hear. Stories like men getting their manhood taken away and who was toughest at which prison, etc. Each talking louder to prove their points and boost up the people they thought to be bigger gangsters.

As I sat in my seat, still wearing my grey two-piece suit, brown suede shoes with my sack bag full of old letters, one of the men began to question me about who I was and what I had done. After I told him he told me that I was probably going to Jackson or Ionia and that I would probably only do eight of the fifteen to thirty years that I'd been given. At that point I wasn't intending on doing one year much less eight.

After a couple of hours we arrived at our destination. We pulled up to the back of the prison and one of the prison officers got off the bus and went inside. Meanwhile a lot of the prisoners out on the yard started walking toward the fence to see if they recognized any of us. One of the men on the bus started pointing at people he knew while the rest of us pretty much sat in anticipation for what was to happen next. When the officer who'd gone inside returned to the bus he told us to remain seated until our name was called. After our name was called we were led off the bus and to a caged area called the bull pen. Once there they took off our cuffs and then we were directed to sit down on a long wooden bench which was bolted into a brown dingy brick wall that reminded me of the projects. We sat on the bench for about a half hour after which point the officer returned with a tray of brown paper bags each containing a peanut butter and jelly sandwich, a milk and an apple.

After I finished eating, they called me into a small room and ordered me to strip naked. After I went through all the humiliating things that all new prisoners go through; including bending over and opening the crack of my ass, they took all of my worldly clothes and asked where I wanted them sent? I told them to send them to my mother and that was that. We were not allowed to keep any clothing item that we'd arrived with.

After we were issued our prison uniforms, the seven of us were led through a set of gates… each one clinging loudly behind us as we walked through. As we were led through the prison, the noise was very loud. People were yelling, cat calling, and cursing as if this was Northville Psychiatric Institute instead of prison. It sounded like sheer chaos. Everybody was talking at one time and I could hardly understand a word anybody was saying. To say the least I was nervous as hell.

I was led into a cell about the size of a regular size bathroom, but instead of a bathtub there was a bed, a sink and a toilet. As I walked into my cell, the cell door slammed behind me and I looked back wishing it could stay open. I sat on the plastic mattress and looked right out across my cell block directly into another man's cell.

I took the white cotton sheet and the itchy wool blanket that I'd been given and made up my bed. I then walked up to the front of the steel bars and looked out. The sight before my eyes was like a nightmare. I was convinced I'd wake up like I'd had many times before and smell the bacon and eggs cooking and my mom yelling at me from the kitchen to get up and eat. However the longer I stood looking out at this replica of a caged in dog pound, something deep inside told me that this was not a dream. It was the worst feeling that I could ever imagine. I'd become a 20th century slave.

During the rest of August I began a one month quarantine period that included both a mental and physical evaluation. During quarantine everybody starts off at Jackson and then either appointed to stay there or sent some place else. During this period they go over everything with us. Our job options, available trades, drug rehab if needed, etc. It also includes determining whether we're competent enough to withstand the pressures of prison. Of course it doesn't matter whether you can withstand it or not, you're still not going home.

In jail your prison number is your name. When an officer confronts an inmate you must give your number first, and then your first name.

During quarantine, each morning at 7:00 a.m. an officer wakes us by yelling the word, "base", at which time you are to hurry to your cell door because the next sound you hear will be the breaking of the bars. At that point you are permitted to slide open your cell door. If you do not open your door at this point, then it will not open and you will have to stay in your cell until the next point of exit.

When you walk out of your cell, everyone then lines up and heads to breakfast. Just like you may have seen on television, there is an inmate for each portion served. If you do not get everything you want to eat the first time around, that's it. There is no going back. Once you sit down, you have a total of ten minutes to eat, after which time you must go back to your cell. Once you get back and the officer yells, "Breaking fourth-catch your doors", you better be in your cell or you are issued a misconduct ticket. The misconduct for missing your cell door is called "out of place." Now no matter what your reason is for not being in your cell, you will still get a ticket. There are no excuses for being out of place.

By 8:00 a.m. your bed must be made up or you are issued another ticket. Once each cell is checked and is confirmed clean everyone in the west section is then allowed to go to the yard. The east goes in the afternoon.

At this point you can either go to the yard or use the telephone. We are only allowed an hour out of our cells so everybody is moving real fast. By 11:00 we must be back in our cells or yes…another ticket.

Basketball is the big thing out on the yard. It's also a proving ground for a lot of the new inmates. It's the first place a new inmate is tested. You are tested for toughness, your ability to play, as well as your ability to stand up for yourself as a man. Many guys play basketball just to prove their toughness. They could care less about the game.

After the 11:00 a.m. count which generally ends about

11:40 we are then freed for lunch. Once again we only have 10 minutes to eat and then it's back to our cells. After that, the next big thing to look forward to is the mail. It's amazing how wonderful a simple white envelope can change the course of a person's day. Just a hello from momma, what's up from a friend, or a…I still love you Boo from that special girl.

After dinner, which ends at 6:30 pm, that's it for food until the next day, so you can prepare yourself for a long night of tossing and turning. You can forget about walking back and forth to a refrigerator in this place.

Also, after dinner is when the real chaos starts. Everybody has a story to tell and every inmate wants to tell their story at the same time. Everybody is eager for attention at this point and must prove that they were the greatest gangsters since Al Capone. Let everybody tell it they were all big drug dealers and all of the small time drug dealers and big time users were still on the streets.

During this first stage of prison, new guys do a lot of crying. Being locked up is a big adjustment. It's at this point you realize that you're not going home and that bit of realization is generally quite hard to take. It's sort of like going through an entire bad dream and finally realizing that it's not a dream at all.

It's at this point that a lot of guys find God.

After my quarantine period was up I was assigned to Ionia State Penitentiary. I along with fourteen other guys were rounded up, chained together and herded onto another bus.

Once on the bus the horror stories about Ionia began.

For the next hour all I heard was how tough people were, who had killed who, whose manhood had been taken and how the average person could never make it there. By the time we got there I was sick to my stomach. I honestly did not want to get off the bus.

Chapter Two

Before we arrived at my destination, we dropped off a few people at a prison called M.T.U. Some of the men who stayed on the bus with me were bragging about how nice this prison was on the inside. But that bit of information didn't do me any good. I could care less.

We weren't there long before the officer who'd gotten off, got back on the bus. He stated that Ionia was the next stop. As we drove toward the prison, sex became the primary topic. Let the men on the bus tell it, they were all ladies men. The guys claimed to have lots of women, and each claimed to be a hard core dog. Nobody showed any inclination of being soft, but of course we all know that in the real world it's not as simple as merely just talking about how hard you are. Some women will take a guy through more changes than any prison guard ever could. I read just recently where a guy shot his wife and then killed him self. If he were on the bus he probably would have been talking about how hard he was too.

As we continued on, I felt a sense of relief that at least I wasn't white. It seemed like they didn't get any respect in prison. The one white guy on the bus with us looked like he was gonna throw up at any moment. All he heard during the whole ride was how he was gonna get raped and how he'd better know how to fight. I can't tell you what he was feeling as he rode toward Ionia with a bus full of black shit talking hard core criminals, but it couldn't have been good.

The man who was handcuffed to me, like myself, had never been to prison. You could tell that all the talking was getting to him because at one point during the ride he told me that we should stick together when we got to the prison, that we should watch each other's back. That seemed like a pretty good idea to me. I at least had one person who was ready to throw down with me if need be.

When we arrived at Ionia I looked at the big castle looking place and got the creeps. Everything about it was grey and spooked and seemed to have a big dark cloud hovering over it.

As we stepped off the bus, a strange feeling came over me. Oh I know... its called depression. It was a feeling I would not be able to shake for the next fifteen years.

Anyway, we stepped off the bus and was herded into the control center where we were checked into the prison. The officer at the desk asked the officer who drove us if there were any ass holes on the bus and he pointed out two people. The officers both then laughed, then the transport officer turned and headed back to Detroit. I wondered what that was all about. After that we were escorted to the chow hall. On the way to chow, a few of the prisoners started giving goo goo eyes to the female officer who was leading us to chow. She was a somewhat nice looking lady who by the look in her eyes wasn't up for any bullshit. I did everything within my power to focus and not pay any attention to her, so when the guys would say something and she'd look back, I would feel somewhat embarrassed and avoid eye contact.

When we reached the hall I was just relieved to see food. Most of the inmates in line and in the chow hall were looking to see if anybody knew anyone however at that point I just wanted to eat.

After we ate, we were taken back to the control center, at which time we were given our cell numbers. I was given the number, J-3 cell 11 and the guy that I'd been chained to was sent to J-2 cell 44.

On the way to our cells we walked through an area for trouble makers called detention. It was a dark gloomy area of the prison and you could barely see the men. All you could really see were shadows. As we walked through one of the men asked where we'd come from and somebody in line shouted Jackson. The guy then stated that we should have stayed in Jackson because there was no place worse than Ionia. Then other men started yelling and asking if certain friends of their's was in Jackson. When one of the guys in line tried to answer one of their questions, the officer leading the way cut him off and told him to be quiet. At that point all the guys locked up started yelling and cursing at the guard but all the guard did was kept walking as if he didn't even hear them.

After walking through that area we arrived at our final destination; J-block. As we walked in a lot of guys were wrapped in towels and walking back and forth to the showers.

We were directed up a set of stairs and ordered to check in with the guard on duty. As I reached my floor two white male officers and a very attractive young black woman met me at the desk. I was really depressed during this time and thought it disgusting to see so many people in a good mood. Inmates were laughing, joking with the guards, and pretty much acting like they weren't locked up. I didn't want anything to do with laughter. All I pretty much wanted to do was cry if anything.

After checking in and picking up my supplies, I was led past a group of neatly kept cells. Each had among other things a television, a radio and various magazines. When I got to my cell I looked in and took a deep sigh. There was no television, or radio. I would have to buy my own items of entertainment. The only thing I had was a toilet, sink, desk and a bed and the things I had in my arms which were two blankets, two sheets, two towels, two wash cloths, two pairs of underwear, two t-shirts and a pair of pants and a shirt.

The first thing I did was put away my items. I then made up my bed, after which point I flopped down onto it, put my hands up to my face and started crying. But before I could really get into it, the female officer from the front desk was standing at my cell calling my name. I looked up, at which point she handed me a rule book and then asked if I wanted to use the phone, which I did. She then stated that when the person who was using the phone was finished that she would unlock my cell and I could use it. As she walked away I proceeded to thumb through the book. I couldn't really focus on it too much because I really couldn't wait to use the phone. After waiting for about a half hour, my cell door opened and I hurried to the phone to call my mother.

When I got my mother on the phone, she seemed more concerned about me than I did for myself. She told me to try and stay out of trouble and that she would come to see me as soon as she could. When I finished talking to her I called my girl, who re-assured me that she would stand by my side and be there with me every step of the way. That was really good to hear, however it would be a long fifteen years, and to expect her to really mean what she was saying at the time turned out to be a bit unrealistic. But for the time being, I held on to every word.

After I hung up I went back to my cell. As I sat on the side of the bed I couldn't think of anything but home. Home was all I'd ever known at that point and it would consume my mind for quite some time before I'd learn to accept my fate.

At 6:30 p.m. my cell door opened again. This time it was accompanied by a voice on the loud speaker announcing yard time. As I stood looking out of my cell guys were rushing past, however unsure about what to do, I remained in my cell. After a few minutes my cell door closed and I sat back down on the bed.

No sooner had I sat down a guy that I'd known from the neighborhood walked up to my cell smiling. His name was King. I used to hang out with his twin brother. I was surprised that King knew I was there. Not only that but he knew what I'd been convicted of also. The only thing that he didn't know was how much time I'd gotten. When I told him fifteen to thirty he told me that I wouldn't have to do the whole thirty, that I would probably only end up doing about eight years. He then said that he'd been there for eight years already and was looking forward to getting out soon. When he told me how long he'd been in prison I almost fainted. I couldn't imagine doing that much time and here this guy was looking happy, positive, and healthy. I didn't want to look like that. I didn't want to be in prison period. The only way I wanted to look was down and out, depressed and miserable. But I had to stay focused. I couldn't let this guy know how down I was so I put up a front. I tried to act upbeat. He asked if I needed anything and I told him I needed some bare essentials, like soap, something to read, and something to snack on. He then told me he'd be right back and returned shortly with everything I'd asked for. It's funny because I would later find myself doing the same for countless people during the next fifteen years.

King even got the guards to let me out to take a shower. When I got to the showers, which looked pretty much like those we used back in high school, the craziest part about the whole thing was that a female guard stood watch over us. That was something that I definitely couldn't understand. With all the men in the world and no women for us to date, they had a woman watching a bunch of naked sex crazed prisoners take showers. It seemed like none of the other men had a problem with it, but I sure did. I didn't need that in my life. I was actually pissed about it.

Later on that night, as I sat on the side of my bed, I was finally able to break down without interruption. It was hard to accept that I could not simply get up, open that cell door and go home.

After a couple of weeks, with the help of my family I was able to purchase a radio, television, tape player and other personal items. Compared to mine, many of the prisoners really had nice looking cells. Many looked like small apartments.

Ionia is a close custody level four prison. That means that dangerous men that must be closely watched are held there. There is only one level worse. That's maximum security. In maximum security prisons you are locked down 23 hours per day. At our level we are allowed some freedom during the day. In lower level prisons like level three the inmates can stay outside for most of the day if they wish.

My day started at 7:00 each morning with breakfast. After breakfast I attended school. I was placed in the 10th grade. School was not much different from my high school. The main difference was that back in high school, there were a lot of people destined for prison, and of course here they had achieved that goal. Each class was filled with murderers, rapist, armed robbers and the like. Some people were really into trying to get an education while others could care less. You're in a classroom with about 21 men. Some men had one year terms, some had five years, some ten years and some life with no chance for parole. When you first get to class it's totally out of control. People talking and yelling. It's pretty much like your fourth grade class until the teacher walks in and takes control. In prison it doesn't take but a second for the teacher to take control. When he slams his hand on the desk and says quiet. It gets quiet. No one wants to get kicked out of prison class. I mean, where else can you go but back to your cell.

It was because of school that I began to feel that I could stomach prison without committing suicide. At least I was learning how to become a disciplined student, which was something I'd never done in the past.

As negative as I was about prison when I went in, I soon discovered that it did have a lot to offer. School, work, counseling and medical facilities were among the most important.

One of my recommendations from the court was that I had to attend school. So I attended school from 8:00a.m. to 3:00p.m. Like high school, there is always one guy in class looking to make trouble and this place was no different. One day I wore a nice sweat suit to school, and this guy from Flint, who'd been in prison for over 4 years, thought he'd attempt to instill a little fear into me. So on this particular day during recess, we were all standing outside the trailer and this dude walks up next to me and stands and lifts his head up like he's the most important person on earth. All of a sudden he put his foot next to mine as if measuring my shoe size. Then he said how much he liked my shoes and how he'd like to have them. At this point I got real defensive and told my man to back up off me. That I wasn't nobody to be playing with so unless he wanted to get fucked up that he needed to get away from me. He then looked at me, eye to eye, and I guess he noticed that I was serious because he slowly walked on away mumbling. Just that quick he started acting like he was just trying to be my friend and didn't mean any harm but I was pissed. For the remainder of the day I resented the fact that I hadn't gone toe to toe with the guy.

In Michigan prisons, you have only a very few men that stand alone. Everybody else is either a part of some click, organization or religious affiliation. Growing up, I had always heard of Christians, Catholics, Muslims, and Jehovah's Witnesses', but in prison they had those groups and more. They have the Moorish Sign Temple of America, the Mobites, founded by the Prophet Noble Drew Ali, whose motto is the enlistment of black humanity, peace, love, truth and freedom. To be considered a Mobite, you must change your slave name to El or Bey and come to understand that togetherness is the key to unity. They will not accept being called black, Negro or nigger and do not eat pork and hate all white people. A white man is considered the devil and they blame the white man for close to each and every problem that affects black people present, past and future.

Then there are the Malanics. Their prophet is the strong ex-slave renegade, Nat Turner. All Malanics change their last name to X. All militant organizations and religions have one thing in common. To bring black men together for the purpose of fighting against white hypocrisy and the advocacy for black self reliability. Now in prison, each religion thinks theirs is the best so unfortunately instead of everything being positive, like it was intended, there are constant conflicts. As a result I decided to remain independent and true to the one person I knew I could rely on. Myself.

Work also became an intriguing part of my first few months at Ionia because there was one job that really paid a lot of money and most everybody wanted it. It was the prison factory job. Income at the factory could range anywhere from $60.00 to $150.00 with bonus pay at the end of the month. Money like that could allow inmates to not only take care of themselves but also their families. Those that worked in the plant carried themselves entirely different from the other inmates. They had a certain amount of pride in themselves and really took their jobs seriously.

King worked in the factory and informed me that if I got my G.E.D. that he would talk to his boss about getting me in. He stated that although everybody at the plant did not have a G.E.D., that it was a part of the qualifications for getting in so I should get to work.

Whenever I'd see King, he'd always ask me if I wanted to smoke a joint. He seemed to always have weed and was always offering it to me. Drugs are something that flows through prison like water. It might seem surprising to some people but I've seen up to a pound of weed while in prison.

I didn't smoke weed and even if I did I probably wouldn't have been interested. My mind was focused on one thing and that was on trying to get home. During this time I was quiet and stayed to myself. I spent a lot of time in the library trying to find holes in my case and other than that and school, I stayed in my cell. I met some very intelligent men in the law library. Men who had been in prison twenty, twenty five years. It amazed me once again how anybody could do that much time. I was told numerous stories about men who'd gotten out of prison by using the library, so after my first visit, I realized that the library might be my only means of getting home.

When I first started going to the library I could never understand how every inmate in prison wasn't in line to get in. I'd watch them playing basketball, gambling, or just lying back in their cells and I would be amazed. Why weren't they working to get out? Didn't they want to go home?

Well, as much as I tried to focus on the positives and stay away from any potential trouble, I received my first ticket only three months after entering Ionia. It happened one night as a female guard was walking past our cells and a group of guys began bombarding her with soap. I got up to see what was going on and as I did another guard saw me standing at my cell door and accused me of being among the trouble makers. I was subsequently found guilty and confined for about twenty days to detention. It would be a hard lesson of simply being in the wrong place at the wrong time. I hadn't even been in the place long enough to establish relationships, was doing everything in my power to act right and stay out of trouble and yet here I was being placed out of regular population and into a dirty nasty cell with no soap, toothpaste or toothbrush.

While in detention I learned a lot more about the prison. My next door cell-mate, a guy called Dew-Rod spent a great deal of time telling me about the drugs, sex, and level of gambling that permeated the prison.

Detention is the lowest form of jail. The craziest thing about my experience in detention was that I was still going through the process of working on being positive and increasing my self esteem and yet here I was already in isolation. I received quite a few letters while in detention and that along with Dew-Rod helped. One of my friends who was locked up with me named Craig sent over candy bars, as well as other items that I could sell, and a female friend, Margaret kept my spirits up with motivating letters.

In prison, receiving mail is probably the most important part of one's day. It's the closest thing to having any kind of contact with the outside world and also the closest thing to seeing grown hard core criminals act like little kids on Christmas day. It just feels good to receive mail. I will always be grateful to everybody who ever sent me anything.

Like prison, when I was sent to detention I thought it would be a short temporary thing and I would quickly be sent back to population. After all I hadn't done anything wrong, however that would not be the case. I was subsequently found guilty of the soap throwing incident and sentenced to 30 to 60 days in the hole.

When I arrived at the hole, which is basically a dark dingy

corridor with filthy jail cells located on each side, I'd finally reached the very bottom of the pits of hell. If I ever thought up to that point that I would achieve any kind of success in my life, walking into that cell put my entire life into perspective. I was a failure. I was being placed in the lowest most disgusting part of planet earth. The hole!

When the guard locked the cell door behind me, I walked over to the bed and stared in disgust at the filthy mattress that I was expected to lie on. I flipped it over hoping that it would be cleaner on the other side, however it was even dirtier. It looked like a thousand men had lay on it over the years and had pissed, jacked off, and dropped all kinds of food on it. I almost threw up at the mere thought of knowing I would have to sleep on it.

As my eyes adjusted to the darkness, I looked up to notice that a bulb was in the socket but it was not lit, so I stood on top of the bed and screwed on the light. What I saw at that point brings images of disgust to me even till this day. There were so many bugs crawling around in that room that I felt like the intruder. I sat down on the side of the bed and put my hands up to my face and rocked back and forth like I was in a mental institution instead of jail.

As I sat going through my mental torment, a person's voice interrupted me. I looked up to see a hand with a mirror sticking into my cell. It was the guy in the cell next to mine. He asked how I was doing, my name, and then asked if I had a match, which I didn't. At that point I guess it was just a relief just to hear another person's voice because being down in that dungeon was terrible. It was kind of like being 5 years old and being down in your grandparent's dark basement at night without an adult. I also didn't have any of my stuff at this time so I was pissed even more. I'd asked the guard if he would bring them to me, which he said he would, however he took his time doing it and had a very bad attitude when he walked passed my cell and I reminded him of it. The pipeline among security was that I had thrown soap at one of their own and so every one of them took it personal. I understand that most people have probably never gotten accused of something that they didn't do by the police, but for those of you who have, I'm sure that you can relate. It's bad enough that you're already in a place that you are being held against your will, and then to get treated like a maggot, like a disgusting insect, there can be no worse feeling.

Imagine being in a relationship and the person that you love tells you out of the blue that they don't want to be with you anymore. That they've found someone else and there is nothing that you can say or do to change their mind about leaving. Now imagine feeling ten times worse...

After what seemed like hours, but was really only about a half hour, an inmate brought me two sheets; two blankets, a towel and a wash rag, but no pillow. After I complained about that to the officer who later brought my bag, which contained my personal items, he stated that I would have to get one from the morning shift.

The following morning an inmate showed up at my cell with my breakfast as well as 5 candy bars, 2 packs of gum and an envelope from Craig. The envelope contained 10 stamps along with a letter informing me that he'd told my family about my predicament. Basically reassuring me that if I needed anything that he had my back. All of the stuff that Craig smuggled to me was illegal. If I or the guy who'd given it to me would have gotten caught, we both would have gotten major tickets. The hole was meant for one thing; unconditional punishment.

Later on that morning I also discovered another very uncomfortable thing. Located right next to my cell was the yard. It wasn't a big yard like the main one however when the guards would open the door leading outside, the cold air would rush right into my cell. I had no heat, a thin blanket, and nothing except cold bars in between me and the freezing cold.

When one of the officers walked passed my cell, I asked if I could talk to her about my situation but she simply looked at me like I was a roach and kept walking. She did yell back over her shoulder that she would be back, but she never did return. I ended up later asking another guard if I could be moved and he said that he would see what he could do.

I was later moved down the hall to a heated cell. That was a relief, however the same day that I was moved, my old neighbor with the mirror got into it with a few of the guards. As it turned out the guard that had given him the ticket that caused him to go to the hole had walked passed his cell and he'd challenged her about why she'd set him up. He'd basically asked her why she hadn't given him the benefit of the doubt. One thing led to another and the next thing we knew he was being dragged yelling and screaming out of his cell.

In the hole, everything is cut in half. Your toothbrush, ink pens...anything that can cause a choking hazard is cut in half before being passed out. So as I brushed my teeth after the neighbor incident, I wondered what my fate would be relative to doing my time in the hole.

My new neighbor was a hard guy who'd been detained in the hole for being disrespectful to officers. He was an alright guy though. He told me that after about thirty days that I would be allowed to bring my television and radio into my cell. He also told me that the officers were foul and disrespectful and that he had been in the hole for six months. He'd caught a ticket because he'd woken up early one morning and had accidentally bumped his food tray and it fell on the floor. For that he was accused of throwing his tray at an officer. Like me, he'd tried to explain how that wasn't the case, but to no avail. It was good having this guy to talk to. Being in the hole alone can be a very draining experience. Just having someone who understands makes all the difference in the world.

What amazed me more than anything about prison during my first few months was how crooked the employees of the system were. They spend all of their time acting like the prisoners are the worst people on earth, yet they lie, deceive, and could give less than shit about treating us like anything except less than human.

For example, when my bag with my personal items was brought some of my clothing was missing. When I brought this up to the counselor I had to go through hell and high water just to prove that I was telling the truth. I had receipts for my clothes and yet I still wasn't believed. I was framed to get to the hole and then once in the hole my clothes were stolen. It seemed like both of my neighbors had also been framed or found themselves in situations where the officers had overreacted. Who are these people that seem to take great joy in other people's misery? Are these the kind of people that we should feel confident in helping to change the course of our prison system. Prison is supposed to be about rehabilitation not retaliation. How can we be expected to change and become productive people once out of prison when those who run the prison system are not willing to stick by their guns and uphold the principles that they swore to when taking office. How is it that we are not expected to quit when it comes to remaining positive and believing in ourselves when it seems that many employees of the prison system have stopped believing in the possibility for positive change. They have seemingly stopped believing that rehabilitation is a possibility and instead have joined the mentality of criminals and began to act like criminals themselves.

I never did get my missing items, however I think I've made my point.

The day that my television was brought to my cell was a

very happy day. It was such a relief to have the opportunity to see my favorite sitcom, "Family Ties" again. That was my favorite show and no matter what the show was about it would make me laugh. Having a simple thing like a television really made us feel like real people. It made it more like home. It didn't matter how filthy the place was or how evil the officers were, just having such simple pleasures made life all that much easier.

After awhile me and my new neighbor, Dollar Bill became real close. You'd be surprised at how innovative you can be when locked up behind bars and also how close you can become to total strangers simply because of one's predicament.

After being locked up next to Dollar Bill for about a month, he was transferred to Marquette. As soon as I was beginning to adapt to the hole, they transferred my new best friend. I was sick.

The other inmates tried to make friends with me and get me to play chess with them, but my heart just wasn't in it. I couldn't muster the strength so I pretty much occupied the rest of my time watching television and listening to music.

The one upbeat time came on the night of New Year's Eve. At midnight everybody started yelling and cheering and throwing paper out of their cells. It was the one time that we were allowed to act a fool and not end up getting a major ticket.

After about 90 days I was sent back to population. Amazingly, by the time I was sent back to population, I was pretty comfortable with being in the hole and really didn't care. It was all the same to me. I was a prisoner with no place else to go.

A few months after getting placed back into population I was called to the counselor's office. Whenever a prisoner was called to the office, you never knew if it was regarding snitching, a ticket, or something relative to home.

I knew I hadn't done anything wrong, but that didn't always mean anything. I'd been down that road before.

When I reached the counselor's office, the guy was a lot more compassionate than normal so I knew something was wrong. Before he even went into what was wrong he asked me if I was alright and that I probably needed to sit down. I searched his expressions for any possible clues but I could come up with nothing. I wished that he would stop stalling and tell me what the problem was because the anxiety of waiting was getting the best of me.

Finally however, he broke down and told me that my grandmother had passed. I was shocked. Being that I was in prison, it was bad enough that unlike most grandchildren, I could not visit. Therefore the news was even more traumatic. A million thoughts went through my mind; however the one that brought tears to my eyes was knowing I could not be there with her on her death bed. I got up and walked blindly back to my cell. I loved my grandmother. I wanted her to see me do well in life, but now here I was walking back to my jail cell- a fallen man with 15 years of prison time yet to do. By the time I reached my cell I could not hold back the pressure. I sat down on my bed and broke down like a baby. It was the simple things that got to me. Not being able to run to the store for her. Not being able to take out her garbage, to cut her grass, or mop the floor. To simply hug her and tell her how much I loved her.

Instead the only thing that I probably brought to her last days was the grief and disappointment that she surely felt as a result of my incarceration.

On my way back to my cell I'd run into Craig and told him what had happened. Other prisoners were really good about relating to death because everyone realized the same thing; there is very little that we can do to help ease the pain of our love ones. We can call home, which with the help of Craig getting to the phone first I was able to do, however we can't be there. We can't take charge. Make arrangements. Be the man of the house. All of that penetrates our souls like arrows to the heart. It's a very painful and humbling experience.

A few weeks after her death, as if that wasn't enough, I was given notice that I was being transferred to another prison. M.C.F. This was very upsetting news. I didn't want to go. I'd made friends where I was. Craig was like a brother to me. He'd become my best friend. What was this new place? The inmates said that it was nice. That it had a big yard, 10 speed bikes and one man rooms. But I didn't care. I felt like a slave being purchased by a new master. I would have to leave the plantation and go some place that I knew nothing about. Man what a life.

Chapter Three

The bus arrived to pick us up around 9:00 a.m., the month was February, and the year, 1986. I was shackled at the legs and hands and led onto the bus with about six other inmates. As I sat back for the four hour ride, I wondered how I would cope with being handcuffed for such a long period of time. Being handcuffed for five minutes was too much for me. I would have to eat this way, sleep this way as well as use the bathroom. I'll tell you, this was one ride I was not looking forward to.

When we arrived at the prison, the rule was when the officer with the paperwork called our names, we were to stand up, give our number, say our names and step off of the bus. Once off the bus, an officer checks your name and number again, and then he takes the handcuffs and leg chains off.

After only eating a sandwich, orange, cookie and milk for the whole ride it was more than a relief to hear the phrase, line up for chow. We walked passed all the staring prisoners who'd lined up to greet us and headed to the chow hall. From the outside the hall looked like a McDonald's. In fact, the entire place looked like a college campus. The housing units were clean, the grass cut, and the trees trimmed. As I looked around, I immediately noticed that a lot more blacks worked at this prison as opposed to the last one.

It didn't really matter what color the guards were though,

the blacks didn't treat us any better than the whites, however I did make a mental note of the difference.

When we reached the front of the line, another big difference was the prisoners serving us asked what we wanted to eat, as opposed to Ionia which simply slapped the food on your plate and sent you on your way. I simply assumed that it was that way at every prison. After eating, we were taken to the waiting unit. There, guys were walking around in pajamas and robes. If not for the mental state of knowing that we were in prison, you'd thought we were in a nice hotel complex somewhere.

As we stood at the front desk, they called our name and number and asked if we smoked. After confirming whether we smoked or not we were then given the keys to our rooms, as well as directions on how to get there. My room number was 19. When I got to my room I was pleasantly surprised. I unlocked the door, walked in, closed the door, then opened it and walked back out into the hall.

As I stood feeling out my new home, one of Craig's good friends, a guy name KB spotted me and called my name. He told me that when I finished doing whatever I was doing to come up and check him out. That he was in room 34. Even though I didn't really know KB that well, he was nevertheless excited to see me. You would have thought we were great friends. Even before I could get myself together and get to his room, he sent this dude to my door who instructed me to meet K.B. in the T.V. room. So I put my property up, locked my door and headed to the T.V. room. When I got to the

35

T.V. room K.B. handed me a bag full of personal items. The bag contained about ten dollars worth of stuff. It was great to receive such a warm welcome. K.B. was from the west side and I was from the east side so it was really unusual for west side guys to show a person like me love like that. Generally the only time that you saw that was when Detroit guys were far away from the city and therefore had no other choice but to stick together.

After about a month of having my own small apartment, I was transferred over to a section of the prison called the gym. The gym was a wide open space with bunk beds. There was no privacy and you really had to watch your property because by it being wide open like that, the minute you turned your back, anybody could rip you off at any moment. This was also my first time having someone sleeping so close to me. It also was a shock to find out that I was being transferred because when I first got to the prison I assumed I would remain in a room. However prison is what it is. You never quite know what to expect.

In spite of the move however, and as time would show; this did turn out to be one of the best prisons in the system. Not only did we have bikes, but first rate movies were shown every week. We also had tennis courts, a pool room, ping pong tables, in addition to an inside weight pit. The outside grounds were also immaculate.

As relaxed as this prison was however, I had my first fight there. It was over an issue with my clothes. There were two ways to get clothing washed. The first was to group them with everyone else's, after which they would be cleaned by a prison inmate and then returned to you based upon the prison number stamped on your clothes.

The second was to pay a set amount to this same person and you could get your clothes washed separately. The pay was one dollar for a full load or three dollars for a month.

Well, one day I got my laundry back and a shirt was missing. So I went to the guy and informed him that my shirt was missing and could he get it for me. I figured that he would just go get it and that would be it. However when I brought it up to him he got very disrespectful and started talking to me like shit. He told me that I needed to go back and check my mothafucken bag because he didn't have the shirt. I stood there and just looked at this guy, shocked at how he was talking to me. But I went back to my bunk and checked my bag.

After searching real good and not finding the shirt I headed back toward the laundry room. On the way I ran into K.B. I told him about my dilemma and he decided to follow me to help get my shirt. By this time I was furious. Not only did I not have my shirt but I'd been disrespected.

As I approached the guy he immediately started yelling about how he hoped I wasn't about to get in his face about the shirt but before he could finish what he was saying, I walked up to him and punched him right in the mouth. I didn't want to hear it. I hit him twice after which he tried to grab me, but before he or I could really do any damage, K.B. and this other dude broke it up. At this point the guy was really mad. It turned out that he was a Moorish American. When I found that out I got kind of nervous because when you mess with one of them its like messing with all of them. Fortunately for me, K.B. knew some of the guys so acting as a mediator he told me that he would talk to a couple of the leaders and help resolve the problem.

About an hour later as I was coming out of chow I was approached by the laundry man and five more guys. One of the men asked if he could talk to me and before I could respond the laundry guy started yelling and acting crazy like he wanted to see me dead. But being that K.B. had already talked to a few of them they were not as quick to do me in. So this one guy who turned out to be a brother named Thomas Bey Grandshiek asked me what happened. Why was the two of us beefing? I explained that my shirt had come up missing but the real problem was how I'd been disrespected in terms of the way in which I'd been spoken to. As far as I was concerned that was more of a problem than the shirt. I explained to him that all I had was my respect and manhood and if he would have talked to me better and with the proper respect then it would not have escalated to that point.

The brother agreed. Right about this time K.B. and a few other guys walked up and asked me if I was alright, which I was. Thomas-Bey then looked at the laundry man and then at me and promised that the laundry man would get my shirt.

Later that day, another inmate brought me my shirt. He

said that it had been mixed up with his clothes. After he gave it to me I watched as he walked over to the laundry man and explain to him what had happened. Then the laundry man walked over to me and with a real grimy attitude asked if I'd gotten my mothafucken shirt. I looked at him, eye-to-eye and told him that I had in fact gotten my shirt and then apologized for the way everything had turned out. As fate would have it we later actually became friends.

Living in the gym was very uncomfortable. It was like living in a small Project housing unit. Everybody seemed miserable and hated each other. The Blacks hated the whites and the whites hated the Blacks. Many of the guys tried to take their minds off of the situation by going to school or working, while others simply gambled all day. In spite of such alternative escape routes though there was always fights about something.

Sleeping in the gym was a monster, especially at night. All you could hear as you tried to sleep was snoring, farting and people whispering. When the smell of the farts start penetrating your nose, you can't just get up and leave. You also can't tell fifty people to stop snoring and the whispers can literally drive you crazy.

One night I got up to take a piss, it was around 3a.m. and as I staggered to the bathroom I could hear heavy breathing. As I approached I tried to ignore the sounds but curiosity got the best of me, so I peeped around the wall and to my surprise two guys that I knew, and thought were straight, were fucking.

As I said before, in prison, there's a lot going on. My bunkie at this time was a white boy named Young, and at the time, he was a laundry man. Well anyway, some guys had lost their drugs, and Young found it. I didn't know anything about it, but Young started giving me money and buying everything he could get his hands on. After awhile a guy came up to me and asked if Young had popped up with any drugs. At the time I told him no because I hadn't seen any drugs. Anyway, about a week later, a few inmates got a hold of Young and cracked him upside the head with a lock. Come to find out Young was selling the drugs out on the yard and talk got back to the gym.

Now in the process of all of this, Young and I were eating good and spending money, when all the time Young was using me. Soon, the guys in the gym started looking at me funny. It wasn't long before word spread that I had taken the drugs and given them to Young to sell for me. It was K.B. who'd come to me and warned me about what was going on. He also told me that I was scheduled to get my head cracked but the guys wanted to be sure before they cracked open my head. However, they were now on my trail and K.B. needed to know what I knew about the whole thing so that he could try and help.

Come to find out the white boy had set me up. He'd told everybody that he was selling the drugs for me. Of course that wasn't true, but that didn't matter. We were talking about criminals here. People who liked to kick ass first and ask questions later.

When I saw Young I approached him and asked why he

had included me in on his scheme. When he started playing dumb, before I could knock his ass out, K.B. walked up and stopped me. He basically got Young to admit everything and in the process retrieved the remaining drugs and gave them back to the guys that he'd taken them from. K.B. gave them the remaining drugs and explained what really happened.

I came real close to getting beat upside the head with a few metal locks for doing nothing...except being naive.

A few weeks after this episode, I was moved out of the gym and into a one man cell. The unit I was sent to was also the unit where K.B. lived so I was happy about that. He was a real cool guy who knew a lot about how to survive in prison. He was the type of mentor that I not only needed but depended on. He knew the rules of prison life.

I was glad to be in a one man cell again. I laid it out just like a nice apartment. They say the way you lived out in society is the way you'll live in prison. And that's true. You have guys who don't take showers, or wash their clothes. Some people need others to tell them to do such things and if they don't have that, they don't do it.

When I got situated in the room, KB came in and asked if I would hold some money for him. At that time we could have only $75.00 at one time in our account. He gave me a hundred dollars in tokens and told me that he would give me $25.00 for holding it. I put $50.00 up in my locker and $25.00 in three different pair of pants. This went on for about three months. Sometimes he would give me $200.00. I was making so much money, I didn't need anything, and so I started loaning money out. I would give a guy two for one. I'd give him $2.00 and he'd give me $4.00 back. I was doing super well. I was prison rich. I even wrote my friend Craig a letter, telling him how well I was doing and how his boy K.B. was looking out. This place was too sweet. As far as jailing, we had everything, and my name was popular as well, everybody knew that I was KB's mellow. Every day he used to sit me down and school me about prison life and making money. He told me how people would smile in my face and then be the same guys to turn around and stick me up. He warned me over and over about being too open and friendly to people that I didn't know.

K.B. really took me under his tutelage and looked out. I had so much money that I was sending two to four hundred dollars home at a time.

After a while, many of the inmates began to get jealous. A few guys even tried to rob K.B. however when that didn't work, they started to send kites and tell on him to get him off the yard. After that almost at least once a week the officers started shaking me down.

The guys in the yard didn't like him getting money and they began not to like me either.

The shit hit the fan one day while playing basketball. A guy who used to work for K.B. but had now turned against him, ran over and gave me a hard unnecessary foul. So I asked him what his problem was and to be cool. He took it to another level and jumped in my face like he was ready to throw down.

My friend D-El ran over and broke it up and told me to let somebody else take my place. At first I let my pride get to me and I refused to quit. But D-El convinced me that what was going on was about more than basketball and that I should chill. D-El started telling me about the whole play being laid down to get K.B. off the yard and that I was being used as a pawn to help bring him down. He told me that they were about to kill K.B., and because I was his boy they were going to take me out too!

In prison, when they do your friend, it's mandatory to get you too. So now my mind and heart was flipping and moving like a jet. I went and hollered at K.B. and told him what I'd heard. He told me that he already knew and was therefore about to make a move to get transferred before the hit went down. He then gave me $400.00 in tokens and the names of some guys who owed him money. He told me that after he left I would be straight and not to worry. That the hit was on him and the only way they would fuck with me was if we were together. And with that, K.B. lit a joint, got busted smoking it, and was shipped to the hole where he remained until being transferred to another prison.

A lot of guys were glad to see K.B. leave. Others were equally glad to see me now standing alone. The word quickly spread as to whether I could survive without him. Even I was somewhat doubtful about my standing; however I knew I had to stand strong. I didn't have much of a choice. This was prison and the first sign of weakness and its over.

My first test came when I had to collect from this guy named G. He owed K.B. some money and I'd already asked him for it a few times when I decided that I had to make a stand. Other people were paying me but this one guy just would not pay me. Every time I asked him he had an excuse. So one day I approached him and told him that if he didn't have the money to pay me he needed to take off his watch and ring and pay me with that. Of course it didn't come out as nice as it was just written and I was damn serious about him giving it to me. His debt was $300.00 and I was not about to let him get away without paying. He'd told me over and over that he'd sent the money to K.B.'s wife but every time I would call her and ask her about it, she'd say that no money had arrived. So by the time I demanded the jewelry I was pissed. I just walked up to him, smacked the shit out of him and demanded the stuff. He was totally caught off guard. To tell you the truth I was just as surprised as he was that I'd smacked him. But he took the stuff off and gave it to me. I told him when she received the money he could have his ring and watch back and then walked back to my cell.

Of course the next day as violence would have it I was sitting in my room and heard a tap at the door. When I answered it there was a group of guys standing there. Tough, hard, ugly, mean mothafuckas. It was actually just two guys and G but they were so big and tough it felt like a whole gang. One of the guys demanded that I give his cousin back his watch and ring and who did I think I was calling myself colleting on K.B.'s debt.

I told him that I wasn't giving him shit and that when I got my money he could get his stuff and I walked on passed the guys like they weren't there. Of course I was nervous as hell as I walked away but I didn't have any choice but to stand my ground. My whole thing was that G hadn't said anything as the trio was standing there so if he didn't have the heart to step up and take it from me I wasn't going to allow anybody else to do it for him.

Now by this time, I'd hooked up with D-El. He was a lifer with a reputation for not taking any shit so I felt that I wouldn't have to deal with the situation alone because nobody wanted to fuck with D-El. So anyway, I told D-El what happened and when he saw head later that day, he called him over and asked him why he was fucking with me. I must tell you that I was in awe at the way this guy respected D-El. He'd went from this shit talking hard core mothafucka he was when they'd had me helmed up to the nicest guy you'd ever want to meet. And just that quick the situation with those guys was over.

After that D-El and I became even closer. It seemed like everybody wanted to become my big brother after that. D-El even tried to talk me into becoming a Mobite, an Islamic religion headed by the prophet Nobel Drew Ali. So I looked into it and studied it intently. I never actually joined. But I did study it.

As the months went by, D-El and I became the best of friends. Things were really going smooth for me until one day,

I was on the phone talking with my sister and this guy walked up and demanded that I get off the phone so he could use it. As I was talking to my sister he started calling me all kinds of bitches and hoes and telling me how fake I was. Totally embarrassing me in front of my sister. Well I didn't get off the phone but when I did, I went looking for this guy. He was a lot bigger than me, and probably a lot tougher, but I didn't care. My right hand packed a punch and between that and my manhood, I had no other choice but to hunt this fool down. When I finally found him, I walked right up to him, and hit him dead in the eye. I hit him so hard that he dropped to one knee. I hit him a few more times and then two guys ran over and pulled me off of him.

As they pulled me away I kicked him so hard up his ass that he had to tighten his ass cheeks. It shocked everybody at how big this guy was over me. As I walked away everybody started calling me a dog. When the guy, Arnold-El got his composure he was mad and embarrassed as hell. He started yelling how he was going to fuck me up but I didn't care. I'd stood up for my manhood and that was all I was concerned about at that point.

That whole day after I'd walked away and went back to my cell, he kept telling everybody that I sucker punched him and how he was going to kick my ass as soon as he caught me. So one day I caught him in the card room, walked up to him and started beating him upside the head with the end of a broomstick. I busted him up real bad. Blood was everywhere.

On the walls, the floor, his and my clothes... every where. I was intent on shutting this mothafucka up once and for all.

This time there was no denying anything. He balled up and cried like a baby. The other guys at the table were in shock. Here this guy had talked all this shit and now he was getting his ass beat, twice, by a man half his height, and half his size.

After that beating, the guy called a truce and I never had any more problems out of him.

See in prison, when a guy puts out a rumor that he's going to do something to you, you better go to him and clear that shit up right away. Now every situation is different so each situation has to be handled differently. Sometimes, you might get a guy who doesn't talk or tell his business and you'll never know he's after you. In this situation a lot of Mobites would come to me as if they just wanted to know what was going on between me and this guy, but they were really feeling me out; setting me up for the kill. A lot of Mobites are for trouble, their power is in numbers, but I stood firm and told my side and told them that I would die for my manhood and respect. He'd disrespected me and all I had was my pride and respect. So I stood firm.

For a few weeks after the truce, life was pretty tense. I never knew if somebody was waiting behind the next corner, waiting to kill me and leave me for dead...all because some dude had demanded that I let him use the phone.

Chapter Four

The year was now 1988 and I had been locked up for 3 years. I was pretty much beginning to accept my fate of being in prison on a long term basis. Nothing had come of any appeal so I began to look more realistically at my future. I was beginning to adjust and at this point was in the swing of things. I'd already been a part of a few good hustles, I was currently running my own store, I had a job as a porter, and my loan hustle was still going strong. I'd managed to build a reputation as a nice guy but one who didn't take any shit off of anybody. I'd been lucky to hook up with the right people…tough no nonsense type of guys who had my back. Most of what I feared coming into prison no longer seemed a problem for me. I felt that as long as I stood my ground as a man that I would be alright.

However, in spite of how well things were going, trouble always seemed right around the corner. That was one thing that was pretty hard to avoid.

During this period, one of my friends, a guy by the name of L.B. got into an argument with one of the officers. The argument got heated and the officer ended up sending L.B. to the hole. After that, D.B. went to the desk and asked the officer why he sent L.B. to the hole. The officer then got real belligerent with D.B. and started talking real grimy to him. He ordered D.B. away from his desk and threatened that if he didn't back away from his desk right then that he would be disobeying a direct order. That would mean a major ticket. So D.B. turned and left. But it wasn't over. He went to his room and packed up all of his property. He then put on his State blues and went back to the desk. The officer thinking that it was over had gone back to his paperwork so when D.B. walked up he wasn't prepared for what was about to happen. D.B. walked right up to the guy and as soon as he looked up hit him in the face with his fist so hard that the guy's glasses went flying clear across the room. D.B. then rushed around the desk and started beating the dog living shit out of him. The officer never had a chance. He talked like he was such a tough guy and now here he was crying like a bitch. Another officer who wasn't too far from the scene ran over to the guard's defense, jumping on D.B.'s back and throwing him to the ground. At that point, D.B.'s homeboy, Dun-El ran over and pulled that officer off of D.B. and the fight was on. Before long 10 officers were swinging and tussling with D.B.and Dun-El. Then two more inmates jumped into the fray at which point D.B. grabbed one of the guards in a head lock and refused to let him go. The sergeant demanded that D.B. let the guy go but D.B. told him that he wasn't letting the guy go until they released L.B. from the hole. That move got D.B. a kidnapping charge on top of the other charges he was now facing for jumping on a prison guard. Dun-El who had been heating up a bowl of grits in the microwave, ran over and got them and threw them on the guard that had started it all. As I stood along with other inmates watching the whole thing, the guard began yelling for help, but there was nothing anybody could do about being hit with a bowl of hot grits.

At this point I ran over and tried to warn the guys fighting that they should calm down before things really got out of hand. But D.B. didn't want to hear anything I had to say. He was going for blood. He didn't care what happened to him and to make matters worse didn't care what happened to the officer he was choking. I thought he would pass out dead at any moment.

At that point one of the officers ordered me back to my room and I turned around and left. Within a short period of time after that a gang of police officers showed up outside of the prison and began calling D.B.'s name on a bullhorn, threatening that if he didn't give up that they would come in and take him down. When that didn't work, they stormed in and overwhelmed the men.

The officers spent the next few days investigating the fight. They questioned everybody that they thought saw anything. On the third day they stormed my room and drug me out like I'd been the one who'd started the whole thing. I was drug all the way down to the hole. Once again I was caught up in the middle of something that I had nothing to do with. Not only did I receive a major ticket, which is supposed to be issued no longer than twenty-four hours after any given incident, I was given the ticket illegally. After they got me to the hole, the Sgt. started reading me the three-day late ticket, which read, "that he observed me hit another officer and that a confidential witness had corroborated this fact."

I couldn't believe it. So I asked for the name of this so called witness. I had six inmates directly say that I didn't hit an officer and I had two officers say that I didn't have anything to do with the incident. Yet I was still issued a ticket, sent to the hole and two weeks later sent back to Jackson for further punishment.

See prison has a point system, so many points will determine your level. One, two, three, four or five. I had level two points, but due to the incident, I was put in level five, the hole, which at the time was 5-block. When me and the other men, who were also sent to Jackson arrived, the guards labeled us as guard haters and prison life as we knew it would never be the same.

They made us strip naked and took everything. I tried to state my case but to no avail. They told me that if I hadn't hit anybody that it was too bad, that I should have. I stated that I only had level 2 points and that I shouldn't be going to the hole, again, so what.

They gave me an orange jumpsuit about four sizes too big and took me to cell 26-second. When the door locked behind me, I just stood in the middle of the floor and put my head in my hands and cried.

After about 20 minutes, I wiped my face and looked around. The toilet had brown water in it with a button on the wall to push to flush. The sink was rusted out and the bed had no sheets, just a blue mattress. Of course it was nasty. The room was no bigger then a regular size bathroom and once again bugs were everywhere. This was not for me at all.

For the first week, I had no sheets or blanket. I constantly asked but the answer was always no. None of the guards wanted to be the one to give an alleged guard abuser anything.

The prisoner next door to me heard how the officers were treating me and one day he jumped up and told one of the officers to give me my damn blanket. That it was mandatory policy that I at least got a sheet. But the officer simply ignored him and walked away.

My neighbor then walked up to the front of his cell and told me to ask for the Sgt. Which I did, but it still took another three weeks sleeping in that condition before a woman guard finally walked up and asked why I was sleeping in that condition. About a half hour later she came back with a bed roll; which is two sheets, two blankets, one pillow, one pillowcase, one towel and one washcloth. Then she gave me a brown bag, which had two small soaps, one half of a toothbrush, and a small toothpaste.

I felt new life. I said thank you about 30 times. She smiled and told me not to tell anybody that she'd given me the stuff and then walked out. I made up my bed, brushed my teeth and washed up in the sink. My neighbor Jabar seemed as happy for me as I was for myself. He told me how happy he was for me and then sent over a book on Islam.

In the hole anything you get in your room to read is a plus, even a week old newspaper, anything to occupy your 24 hours.

When I was finally allowed to take a shower, I had to take off all my clothes, except my underwear, and walk handcuffed with a dog leash around my neck down a long hallway to the showers. If you stopped at someone's bars, the officer would pull the leash or turn around and smack you with the end of it. I felt like a pit bull ready to snatch a niggas neck off. The shower was up in another area of the hole with bars. Once there, they uncuff you, lock you in, and sit there while you take the most humiliating shower of your life.

As I walked back to my cell I noticed a guy had chess pieces in his room. It is law that you really shouldn't look into another man's cell, but that day I guess I couldn't help it. An inmate will curse you out about that or ask you why you're looking in their house? That's disrespectful.

Anyway I made the long walk back to my cell wondering how this guy had gotten a chess set. I also got a chance to see my next door neighbor Jabar. He was a tall brother, with a really hard looking face and sleepy eyes. He saw me and said, "what's up little man?" I then asked him about how to get chess pieces and he told me that when the guard left that he would tell me how to get chess pieces.

After the guard left, Jabar told me that the chess pieces were made out of toilet paper. I then asked how we would get the board and he said by using the back of a writing pad.

Innovative, huh?

The book on Islam was really interesting. I learned some

things that I'd never ever thought about. In addition to Islam, like I said before, there were a lot of religions to pick from. The irony is they all advocate for the betterment of the Black man yet each has a different approach about how to get there.

The hole was a really crazy experience. It had its own rules. The officers had their rules and the inmates had theirs. Guys would talk loud all day, telling stories about people in the free world as well as other inmates. They would talk all day without ever seeing each other. You could tell who had the most respect just by the voice.

This brother named Rabb who was on the second floor of the hole and another brother from the 3rd floor would play chess all day by calling out numbers 12 thru 34 check. One day the guy on the 3rd floor, who by the way was a Mobite, accused Rabb of cheating. They got into a big argument and Rabb called the Mobite a nigger. That's one word that will get you killed in prison. So some of the other Mobite brothers started telling Rabb not to call their brother a nigger but he got mad and said that they were all niggers and that he didn't give a fuck about none of them.

Well, everybody was locked in their cell for 23 hours a day and whenever we did leave our cell, we were handcuffed, and the only time we got the cuffs off was when we got yard.

It was tension in the air and you could hear the Moes plotting in codes. You could refuse yard everyday if you wanted. As for me, I wanted yard because the phones were out there. The phone area was like a little dog kennel; four inmates caged in an area with room for only two people.

One day Rabb came out to the yard and along with me and two other guys ended up in the kennel together. One of the Mobites tried to get in with us to get to Rabb; a slim brother with long braids and dark skin, and when that happened he called for the guards to go back in. After yard, the Moe who was out there called Rabb all kinds of cowards and kept yelling about how soft he was. But Rabb didn't care. He kept talking trash because he knew that they couldn't get to him.

After about four months of being in the hole, with no TV and no radio, I had pretty much adapted and found a way to keep something to read. The one thing that the guards could not keep us from was the law library. By law if we signed up they had to let us go. So I would sign up for the library and keep myself busy by reading a lot of the cases of prisoners who'd come before me. I really enjoyed reading about the cases as well as about Islam. I even learned how to tell time based on the location of the sun. Between the library, Islam, and chess, which I would play at night, my day was pretty much occupied.

After awhile, after the sergeant had somewhat calmed down about why I was in the hole, I showed him my original ticket and pointed out how I'd been treated unfairly based upon the 24 hr. rule of law. In addition, I pointed out how two other officers at the fight stated that I had nothing to do with it yet I was still given a ticket.

The sergeant looked at it real close and I could see in his

face that he was interested. He shook his head and agreed that it was a bad ticket. But then he said that since I'd already been convicted that there was nothing he could do. Meanwhile, Jabar who'd been listening to the whole conversation jumped up and demanded that the sergeant do something about the ticket. He didn't want to hear anything about what he couldn't do. He knew better and demanded that he take the appropriate steps to look into my case. The sergeant paused and promised that he would look into the matter. But I had my doubts. In my mind, the guards couldn't be trusted any more than the prisoners.

Not a minute after the sergeant walked down the hall, we heard yelling and a prisoner calling for the guards. I couldn't really hear what was going on, but come to find out Rabb had shitted and threw it on one of the Mobites. I couldn't predict what might become of Rabb once he was released from the hole, but his future didn't look too bright. In the meantime however, he was intent on giving the Mobites hell.

After being in the hole ticket free for six months they finally gave me my television and radio. It was about four in the morning and an officer showed up at my cell and asked me if I was Long. After I said yes he opened up my cell and sat the TV and radio in my room. I was so happy. Now I really had something to occupy my time. Jabar asked what the guard had brought and I told him. People don't understand how much a television and radio means to an inmate. Not only does it keep a lot of men out of trouble, it keeps you from going insane. The punishment is still a major factor, but to just lock a man up with nothing turns him into a monster. Rehabilitation means change. Change for the better. You can't just treat people wrong and expect him to come out right. It is a proven fact that wrong will not correct wrong. There has to be some right in the equation to make it even.

A few days after I got my stuff back a few guys were sent down to the hole. One of them was K-El. He was also a Mobite. Me and K-El knew a lot of the same people on the outside, and because of that was really close. He also became my daily chess partner. Anyway one morning as we were going to the yard, I got into one cage and K-El got into another cage. I wasn't paying any attention and allowed him to get into the cage with Rabb. It didn't hit me that he was a natural enemy of Rabb. Before I knew it Rabb got his hand-cuffs off and as the officer was taking the hand-cuffs off another inmate, Rabb pulled out a homemade knife and started stabbing K-El. I looked over and K-El still had his handcuffs on behind his back and Rabb was just swinging away. K-El was in shock, he had no idea why he was being stabbed. The officer was yelling for him to stop stabbing the guy but it was too late. As he tried to open the cage, he dropped the keys, leaving Rabb with even more time to do K-El in. All anybody could do was just look in disbelief. K-El was defenseless. Finally after a minute or so, the officer got the cage open and Rabb threw the knife. The officer then handcuffed Rabb and took him away and had the nerve to ask K-El was he okay.

When I got back to my cell, Rabb yelled down to the Mobites to send another one down. If they could have gotten to that man he would have never lived to see another day.

I'm still baffled to this day as to how the guy got a knife in the hole as well as into the cage. That's what I call a magician.

Chapter Five

Learning lessons in prison was a never ending experience. One day a porter came to my cell, basically to clean up and pass out food. Many times porters are nothing more than rats that can't be trusted. So to say the least, inmates don't spend a lot of time dealing with them. Anyway, this one porter use to come to my cell and he seemed cool enough. He'd always have extra bars of soap and so one day we agreed to exchange a few bars of soap for him using my radio. Every day the guy would give me extras of whatever he would have, and I would allow him to use my radio. These extras included food, toothpaste, stamps, and things of that nature. This went on for about three months and I got comfortable with him. Well one day while I was in the yard, I looked up and saw him leaving the hole and the bad part was he had my radio with him. I was yelling for him to leave my radio but it was too late. I told the officer that the guy had my radio and he asked me how he got it. I felt real stupid, because we were not supposed to loan anything out. To make it worse, this guy wasn't even on my gallery. So he ignored me. As soon as I got to my cell, I hollered at the guy in 38, 2nd and he confirmed that the guy had taken it with him. I was fucked up. Jabar told me to put it in Allah's hand and suggested that this would now give me more time to read the Quran. I was so mad that if I could have gotten my hands on that guy I would have snapped his neck in two.

Well, I made it until January with no tickets. One day as I was lying on my bunk an officer came into my cell and told me to pack up. I was going back to population. I said goodbye to everybody and within an hour or so I was heading out. I was taken straight to 11-block, inside the walls. Everybody calls it the "Belly of the Beast!" As I walked through the block my stomach felt like it had rocks in it. When I reached the desk the lady at the desk looked at me and asked for my pass so I handed it to her. She looked at it and looked at me, smiled and asked why I was in the hole. I simply told her that I was in there for fighting. I didn't say who it was with, I just said fighting and left it at that.

She smiled again and said 64-4 gallery. Boy, I didn't like that at all. I don't like heights, they make me dizzy, but I went up there and had to stand in one spot until an officer came to let me into my cell.

As I stood waiting the greatest thing happened. I saw my good friend Craig. I yelled down to him and watched as he too, smiled and waved back up to me. He was just as happy to see me as I was to see him. In prison, friends, mail, and the telephone are all you have so this was a really good day for me.

As I waited for the guard to open my cell, the guy in the cell next to mine asked if I needed to get into my cell. I told him yes and he picked up a stick, stuck it through the bars and opened the door. At that point I didn't know what to do.

I finally walked on in and sat down. As I looked around I was stunned to see that it looked just like the cell I had in the hole but instead of a wall in the back, it was more bars and a thin walkway, called the catwalk.

After awhile Craig came up. It was a great reunion. The first thing he asked me was if I'd gotten the soap and stamps that he'd sent while I was down in the hole. Another lesson learned. Here I was letting that porter use my radio and he hadn't done a damn thing for me. It was Craig all along who'd sent all of that extra stuff.

I could see that the first night's sleep would be long and uncomfortable. At this point I was really wondering if I would make it at Jackson. When the doors locked for the night it didn't make things any easier. I had no television or radio and therefore could do nothing except sit and think. I simply sat on my bunk and thought about the chain of events that had brought me to Jackson. I was an innocent man as far as the incident with the guards was concerned, but that didn't matter now. I'd been transferred to the meanest prison in the State and I had no choice but to accept it and deal with it. No matter what my mind said, no matter how much doubt kept coming up in my mind about dealing with my situation, none of that mattered. The only thing that mattered was that I was a Jackson State Prison inmate.

As I sat trying to isolate myself from the noise around me, I was beginning to feel like I was trapped in the twilight zone. The inmates were all talking so loud that I felt like I would go crazy. It's a noise that only prison inmates will ever hear. It's an uncontrollable mix of name calling, yelling, and shot calling…it's a human zoo.

If you've ever lived some place and experienced a loud neighbor playing music while you were trying to sleep, or constantly arguing with someone, imagine five hundred neighbors all talking and playing loud music while you were trying to sleep.

As I sat trying to figure it all out, the guy in the cell next to mine stuck a mirror into my cell and spoke. He stated that his name was Black. He asked where I'd come from and I told him the hole. I told him I'd just done nine months there and he asked if I'd killed somebody. I then told him I'd gotten there as a result of an assault on officer charges while at Muskegon. He asked if his boys K-Bey and R-P were in the hole and I told him yes. He then told me that he and Craig were cool and that they worked in the factory together. He then started telling me about the officers at Jackson. He told me which officers were foul and liked to write tickets and which ones were okay…which were only a few.

At this point I was really starting to feel pretty good about Black and having someone to talk to. He seemed cool and plus he was cool with Craig.

That first night was one that I'll never forget. Even though I didn't have my own radio, the prison had a small contraption on the wall which turned out to be a radio. With the small earpiece that Black had given me, I mixed up a glass of rusty watered kool-aid, climbed on top of my twin sized bed, got as comfortable as I could, and huddled up to the wall. As uncomfortable as I was, those first sounds of the Dramatics was pure heaven to my ears. I sat in this position for most of the night until my neck and back couldn't take it any longer at which point I fell back onto the bed and went to sleep.

The next morning, I was awakened at 6:00 a.m. by a guy huddled up to my cell whispering for me to meet Craig down stairs for breakfast. I jumped up, wet my face, and headed to the chow hall. I didn't have a toothbrush yet, so I couldn't brush my teeth. When I saw Craig I told him that I didn't have a toothbrush so he would have to excuse my breath. Like the friend he was, he told me to run back up to his cell and use his. So I ran into his cell and brushed my teeth and washed my face.

Going into another man's cell was illegal, so I had to hurry. Being in someone else's cell could mean a major ticket.

The chow hall was unlike any of the others I'd been in during the past few years. This one was dim, dusty and the men all looked like they could kill a rock and to top it off an officer sat high atop everyone in the gun shack just waiting for something to happen. I felt so out of place.

After I got my food, I walked over to the table occupied by Craig and another friend Peanut and sat down. Peanut was real happy to see me. He told me that he'd heard that I was down in the hole and was really looking forward to me getting out. He also asked how much time I'd gotten and I told him 15 to

30. He asked if I'd seen two of our home boys from the hood named Tone and A.B. and I told him no. I told him that I hadn't seen anybody because this was my first full day in population. He then said that he would tell everybody that we both knew to meet me on the yard.

Remember we only had 10 minutes to get to chow and eat so we didn't have a lot of time; however it was really good seeing people that I knew from the neighborhood.

While most everyone else headed off to school or work, I simply went back to my cell and went to sleep. Before long however an officer popped up in my cell and asked if I was going to the yard. I'd been sleep a few hours by this time so I jumped up, wiped the saliva from my mouth and headed to the yard. As I was leaving out I asked the guard about my property. I hadn't seen it in 9 months. I didn't even know for a fact if it was still there. Nonetheless, he told me that he would make sure that I got my property before the end of the day. And with that resolved I headed to the yard.

When I got outside my cell, I almost got knocked down in the stampede. Guys were running past, saying excuse me but before I could get out of the way they'd already brushed passed and disappeared toward the yard. I simply followed the crowd. When I got down to the first gallery this dude that use to date my sister by the name of Big Lou caught my attention. We shook hands and I told him that I was in 64-4 next to a guy named Black. He then asked me about my clothes. After I told him that the guard had promised to get them he told me that he would make sure that I got my property by the end of the day. I still had on my prison blues and I'll tell you I was pretty sick of them myself.

When I got to the yard, I felt like a deer in a lion's den. Everybody was staring at me like I was somebody from another planet. Lucky for me I was with Big Lou. Who you hang with in prison makes all the difference in the world so when guys saw me with Big Lou, all he had to say was this was my home boy and they knew I was cool. Of course by Big Lou being from the east side that also meant that I was from the eastside, too.

Everybody has a different reason for being on the yard. Some come to gamble, some to play basketball, baseball, or run track, and some simply to talk or get some fresh air. The phone is also on the yard so a lot of men rush to the yard to use the phone. In prison everything is considered money; stamps, soap, food, clothes, ass, mouth and tokens, the official money of the prison system.

At Jackson we only had two hours to be on the yard. From 8am to 10am, then its back to your cell.

As we were leaving the yard, Big Lou saw an officer that he knew and they started joking around and laughing. Big Lou asked the officer to look out for me and he promised he would. He took my name and told Big Lou that I would have my property after lunch.

Well, sure enough, I got my property after lunch. I was really happy to see my stuff. I hadn't seen it in nine months.

As I was unpacking, Craig came up and asked if he could see my pictures. I had tons of pictures so for him that was really an exciting time because he knew a lot of the people in my pictures. I also had $65.00 in tokens from the last prison. I asked him if I could spend them and he said I would have to turn them into the counselor and they would put them in my account. I also had about 70 different bars of soap. I gave Craig about 10 bars and then headed to the showers.

When Black saw that I'd gotten my property, he told me to make sure that I put a lock on my locker because if I didn't my property would get stolen. I felt really happy that day until as prison often does my mood was changed against my will. As I sat in my cell enjoying my things my name was called over the loud speaker ordering me to the guard station. When I got there one of the guards informed me that I'd gotten a ticket. Of course I was confused because I hadn't done anything. I'd run into my boy's room and brushed my teeth but nobody saw that, so I was confused. Turns out, I'd missed a call out which means I was being cited for being out of place. I told her that I didn't know that I had to call out. I asked how I could get a ticket without being given proper instructions but she said I should have known. The problem as it turns out was that I should have been given an orientation, which I wasn't.

Missing call out was a minor ticket but yet a ticket nonetheless. A major ticket goes in your file and they take good time away from you and put you on top luck, which means you are on lock down for a few days. Minor tickets do not go in your file, but they can cause you to have to stay in your cell for a period of time.

When Craig came by, I explained to him that I caught a ticket. He said that it was a bunch of crap and that a guy he knew name J.R. could help. J.R. was good at interpreting the law so he assured me that if anybody could help, it was J.R.

When I first met J.R., he looked like one of those homeless men that you see on the street. He looked like he hadn't had a hair cut or shave since he'd become an adult. Nevertheless J.R. knew the rules of the prison. He stated that I should have been orientated within 48 hours of my arrival to the prison. He also stated that if I wanted to get the ticket over turned, that I would have to go before a hearing investigator. Hearing investigators are hired by the department of corrections to defend prisoners. That was fine and dandy but I knew that any correctional employee was probably not going to listen to anything I had to say. Most prisoners were automatically found guilty no matter what the charge, however, I kept the faith

Like I said before, I hated being on the fourth gallery because it was hard for me to keep my equilibrium being so far up. If I could help it, I would never look down and I would walk as close to the bars as possible. Anyway, one day as I was talking to an officer about moving me, a correction official walked up and stated that I had to move a book off the top of my locker. I thought the request was ridiculous. I looked over at the guy's cell directly across from mine and pointed out that he had numerous things on top of his locker. Why should he be allowed to keep his locker stacked but I would have to remove the book from my locker? I felt like the guy was picking on me because I was new so I held my ground.

When lunch was called and I stepped out of my cell, an older guy from the cell that I'd pointed to stepped up to me. He was polite, and said to excuse him but that I should have not pointed to his cell when I was being reprimanded for doing wrong. He was a big muscle bound guy and had on dark glasses. I started to explain myself but he stopped me and in a nice voice simply asked that I not do it again. He stated that I had no idea what he may have had in his cell, that he could have had anything over there and that I should think twice the next time about pointing at someone else. When he finished what he had to say, I apologized and headed to the chow hall. On my way I ran into Big Lou and told him what happened. As soon as I mentioned the name Mr. K.T. he stopped in his tracks and asked if the guy had gotten mad. I told him no. He then explained that Mr. K.T. was one of the most dangerous men in the prison. That he'd only recently killed a fellow prisoner, after he'd already gotten 25 to 50 years in prison for killing someone on the outside. That little bit of information really spooked me because men had been killed in prison over things as small as a stamp, and now here I was pointing out the business of a stone cold killer.

Mr. K.T. and I later became friends. We would bet on college games a lot. After that lesson on prison life I was always quick to think before bringing anyone else into my problems.

Something else interesting happened around this time. I saw for the first time how serious some people were about being called a nigger. Generally inmates that belong to any Islamic religion will check you about using the word. There were a lot of brothers who took it serious, but on the flip side, there were a lot of brothers who didn't give a fuck and felt like they could say whatever to whomever. Well, I was on the yard one night watching a group of guys play basketball. One of the guys playing ended up calling an X-brother a nigger so the X-brother asked him not to call him that. That it was very disrespectful, so please not to do it again. Well the guy decided that he didn't give a fuck and told the guy he would call him whatever he wanted and at that point the Islamic group who'd over heard the conversation surrounded the guy and pretty much beat the crap out of the man. The guy tried to fight back and for that he gets an award but they fucked him up.

The next day, talk was all over the yard about what had happened. Nobody expected to see this guy back on the yard anytime soon. Then out of the blue, this guy walks out on the yard again. Everybody knows that when you get into it with a group like that, that it's always best to lay low for awhile. So when he walked out onto the yard everybody started staring at him like he was crazy. He was real stupid for coming back out that soon. The X-brothers went straight into action. They secured the yard, encircled the guy and this time instead of beating him stabbed him about twenty times. The guy broke away and tried to get away by climbing the security fence but when he did that he almost got shot by the yard guard who thought he was trying to escape. Luckily another guard ran over and discovered that he'd been stabbed. That's the only thing that kept him from getting shot. When the officer arrived on the scene, he had the nerve to ask if anybody saw what happened. At that point everybody started walking away. Being a rat or telling on someone is something that you just don't do. It is law that the officers are your enemy and there is a code of silence between and among the inmates. To be a rat will make your time in prison hard, long and miserable, because no matter what prison you go to, it will follow you the whole time you're in prison.

I tried my best to occupy my time with something productive while at Jackson. I'd wake up at six o'clock, go to breakfast, then to work at seven. At one o'clock I would attend school, then at three head back to my cell until four o'clock count, then at five I would go to the law library until six, and finally the yard until eight. After that I would take a shower and at nine lock down and the next day do it all over again.

One day as I was coming in from school, I heard someone calling my name. When I looked around to see who it was, it was K.B. Man was I glad to see him. He had just been shipped in from Huron Valley. We talked for a minute and he asked me did I have a toothbrush. I hurried to my cell but when I got there my cell door was locked. Black was home so I asked if he could do that little trick with the stick and he said yes. He stuck the stick in between my bars and the cell door popped open.

I was always amazed when he did that and asked if he could teach me how to do it. I then went into my footlocker and got K.B. a tooth brush, tooth paste, two bars of soap, a wash cloth, a bag of chips, cookies, kool aid, 4 soups and a box of crackers. When I gave him the stuff you'd thought I'd given him the world. He was so thankful. After he got himself together we tracked down Craig. Their reunion was even greater than K.B's and mine.

By this time I had been in prison for four years. On one hand I was learning how to survive in prison, but on the other hand I wished I could figure a way to get out. I felt like I was walking in a maze, living a nightmare waiting to wake up. Many nights I would dream I was a free man only to wake up in my cell. The dreams always felt so real and many times it would take a moment for me to regain my composure and the acceptance that I was really in prison.

Selling drugs in prison can work for a prisoner a number of ways. It can also have the opposite affect. Once you become a kingpin, yes you may make a lot of money, but you also create a lot of enemies. This is what happened with K.B. When he got to Jackson guys there knew that he had a hookup on how to get drugs and they immediately went into action. They demanded that he ship drugs in for them and this immediately put undue pressure on him. I told him that I would sell the drugs for him but he told me that Jackson was not a safe place to sell drugs. These guys would kill me in an instant and think nothing of it. He said that the guys in Jackson played for keeps. He told me that Jackson was like walking through the valley of the shadow of death itself. You could kind of get his point as we walked through the chow hall together. If stares could kill, we would have both been dead before we finished our meal.

K.B. was so serious about what he felt that he even had himself locked down in protective custody. I didn't understand why he would go that far just to make his point, being that generally only people who couldn't make it in population would step that low…but then again it wasn't my life on the line, it was his.

Like most inmates that used the library, I spent most of my time trying to figure out how to get my case overturned. I had J.R. working on my case too. One day after a long study session, I told J.R. that I was going to the store and asked him if he wanted anything. He responded by telling me that he would get it. I was new and I didn't understand why every time I offered to get something for him that he would switch things around and offer to go instead. Not only did he offer to get it but every time he would offer he would look at my zipper. This man looked nothing like a gay man but turns out he was gay. Eventually I got mad and went off on him. The law clerk, an inmate named Griffin Bey, called me over. He told me to keep it down and when I explained what had happened he told me that the guy was gay and liked to suck dicks. He also said that I was lucky because this guy had a reputation for getting guys to come to his room, at which point he would knock them out, suck their dicks, then wake them up, knock them out again and then fuck them in the ass. I didn't know how to respond to this bit of information. I left, not really understanding how to react to this problem and not knowing how J.R. was feeling or going to react.

Lucky for me, Big Lou ended up handling the problem for me. He had a good relationship with J.R. and had a talk with him and resolved everything.

Getting back to K.B., after awhile I did see how he had a point. I witnessed numerous violent acts while at Jackson. On one occasion this guy ran past my cell and actually jumped off of the fourth gallery while trying to get away from a group of guys. Another time I witnessed an inmate get stabbed in the neck and yet another time an inmate get stumped by guards and the examples go on and on.

As things would go in prison, a few weeks after K.B. arrived I got notice that I was being transferred out of Jackson. Ordinarily this would have been good news, however I was being shipped back to Muskegon… the place where I was set up and sent back to Jackson.

This had to be a mistake.

Chapter Six

Without much advance warning or time to say goodbye to hardly any of my friends, the next morning after being notified I was handcuffed and herded onto a bus heading back to Muskegon. I didn't understand this move or why it was happening. In my mind it had to be either a setup or a mistake. Most likely a setup.

When we arrived at M.C.F. there were about twenty officers standing out in front of the bus. We'd been locked up on the bus for over four hours and they wanted to shake us up and down again. They un-cuffed us, called out our names and numbers then led us up to the Aspen unit. As soon as we reached the unit two faces stood out from the many looking to see if they knew any of us.

Marcus and Derrick were two brothers that I had grown up with and seeing them was a pleasant surprise. I also saw the guy who took my radio while I was in the hole. I saw him but he didn't see me.

This time, they didn't give me a key and a room. I was put in what we call a fish tank. A big room with about twenty bunks.

Once I got myself together I went outside where I again ran into Marcus and Derrick. I hugged them and they immediately asked which prison I had been transferred from. I told them, at which point we walked around the yard where I shook hands with a number of people that I'd known during my stay at other prisons.

While we were out on the yard I asked Marcus and Derrick if they knew the guy who'd taken my radio and as it turned out Derrick knew him. The two of them locked in the same unit. When I told them what happened they both got pissed off about it. Derrick immediately left the yard in search of the guy. When Derrick walked away, I had it in my mind that when he brought the guy back I was going to smack the shit out of him.

When Derrick and the guy got back to the yard, the whole thing was so funny because he had no idea why Derrick had brought him out to the yard. As soon as he saw me his face went from happy to shock in a matter of seconds. The first thing he tried to do was explain why he had taken my radio but I wasn't trying to hear it. I told him to go back to his cell and bring back something of equal value or I was going to fuck him up. As insurance I had Derrick to go with him. He ended up sending me about eight dollars worth of stuff back.

As we walked the yard, you could hear the guys whispering about me being one of the men who'd taken part in the assault incident. As a result of the scuffle, four of the guys had caught new cases and four of us were issued tickets and given 12 months in the hole. The other four were given anywhere from 20 to 60 years for their part in the encounter so this incident was one that every inmate in the prison knew about.

My new living arrangements were awful. Everything was so tight that if you passed gas ten other people would smell it. After I got my property and brought it back to the fish tank the men there couldn't wait to see what I had. I knew I had to be careful if I intended on holding on to my stuff.

The following day one of the officer's who'd witnessed the fight saw me and reported to her superiors that I was not suppose to be at the prison and just like that within the next five hours I was headed back to Jackson.

I was put into a station wagon with my property and two officers. As we rode, one of the officers asked me what I'd done that had gotten me transferred so fast. I simply looked at him and smiled.

Remember Muskegon was a lot more laid back than Jackson. It is only a level two prison so being shipped to Jackson was supposed to be a punishing act.

When we got to Jackson, the officer removed my handcuffs and put me in a holding cage. I couldn't wait to get my property to make sure everything was there. I waited in the cage for an hour after which time an officer unlocked the cage and led me to my new home. Gallery 58 second. As I walked back into block-11, a lot of guys were surprised to see me back so soon.

The next day after I had breakfast I found one of the guys that I'd worked with and asked him if he could talk to my old boss about giving me my job back. The guy said he would but as I was talking to him one of the craziest things happened. Somebody walked up to him and stabbed him in the chest with a homemade knife. The man who'd gotten stabbed took off running in one direction and the man who'd stabbed him took off in the opposite direction. I wanted to follow the guy who did the sticking, to tell him that I wasn't with that guy, because in prison, if they hit your friend, then like I said before you are next and I wanted to make sure he knew I wasn't his friend. Then I wanted to follow the one who got hit to make sure he was all right and to let him know that I had nothing to do with the stabbing, because it looked like I had set him up. In the meantime because his blood had squirted all over me when he got stabbed, I had blood all over my clothes and if the police saw me like that I would definitely be in trouble.

As I stood in a trance, Big Lou just popped up from nowhere. He asked me what had happened and I tried to explain but I was just too nervous to get it out. It was a good thing that he walked up when he did because within minutes the cops were everywhere. He took the shirt that I had on, put it up under his shirt and gave me his jacket and we walked away. Then he told me that the guy who got plugged with the knife had broken into this guy Pie Man's cell. Pie Man had a prison store and as a result of the burglary put a hundred dollar hit out on him.

After a couple of months I settled in and opened my own prison store. I would buy a lot of things out of the regular store and when other inmates got hungry, they would buy snacks from me. If they got a cookie from me, when they went back to the regular store, they would bring me back two cookies for the one I gave them. Of course I also collected stamps, money, and soap...anything of value.

My best customer was this white boy name Pauley. Pauley had blonde hair, blue eyes and to make matters worse was short and slim. He couldn't read, write or count, so in school, I would make out his store list for him. The gay predators hated when Pauley was with me and whenever I wasn't around, they would be on him like flies on shit.

He was a cool white boy, he would tell me stories about his wife and kids and how the police tricked him because he didn't know how to read or write. He would spend $15 to $20 in my store every week. That was good money, but the gossip and rumors got around that I was fucking him and the inmates started looking at me cross-eyed and crazy. It was worse than being in elementary school. A rumor didn't have to be substantiated, as long as it was out there people took it to be true.

One day while I was in my cell, I heard a lot of yelling throughout the gallery. It turned out to be a group of guys trying to rape Pauley. When he got to class he had red marks all over his face. I sat down and asked him what happened. He smiled and said they had tried to rape him but he had held his own. He couldn't understand why they couldn't accept the fact that he wasn't gay and therefore wasn't about to let anybody fuck him in the ass. According to prison rule, when a black man hangs with a white man, either he's gay or trying to protect him. And when a black man hangs with all whites, he's an Uncle Tom, gay, or sucking their dicks!

To say the least, I was puzzled as to how to handle this situation. I just wanted to yell from my cell and tell everybody that I was not fucking this boy. At lunch, I saw Craig and he told me that he heard the rumor and for me to leave the white boy alone. But this was my friend. I couldn't just leave him alone because somebody told me too. It would be like somebody telling me not to hang with Craig, K.B., or anybody else I wanted to hang with. But this was prison. No matter how much I tried to act like I could do what I wanted, my fellow prisoners were not going to give me any peace as long as I hung with this guy.

It finally came to a head one day when we were in class and the teacher stepped out for a moment. An inmate while trying to make everybody laugh, came up to me and asked if he could dance with my woman, meaning Pauley. I demanded that he get out of my face and when he didn't, I knocked his ass to the floor. Some inmates jumped between us and when the teacher came back into the room, he could have had us sent to the hole; instead he demanded that we drop it. However, as soon as class was over the guy ran out and told everybody that we'd gotten into it because I was trying to protect the white boy.

From that point on, things really started to escalate. The next day there was this huge commotion on the gallery right under mine. I walked out of my cell and looked over at Big Lou. As soon as he saw me he yelled over that Pauley was fighting again. I found out later that a guy had run up in his cell and tried to rape him again. But once again he had fought the guy off.

This time however, in their own twisted way of resolving things, the guards sent Pauley to the hole for fighting. At least, I concluded, he would be safe and for the time being my problems would be over. Man…what a relief.

Many prisoners would fight no matter what the consequences. Just like this situation, this white boy got sent to the hole for trying to protect himself. Nobody cared about why he was fighting, who he was fighting or how close he was to death. He was fighting so he had to go to the hole.

On another occasion, I witnessed a guy who actually had an out date and had been paroled; but for the sake of his manhood, reputation and homeboys, stabbed a man in the chow hall…right in front of the police. He's still in prison today.

After the incident in the chow hall, I went to my cell and thought about how easy it was to die in prison. I wondered if I had an out date if I would fight for my homeboys Craig and Big Lou. One side of me said yes, but the other side wasn't quite so sure. I guess I would have to wait for something to happen before being put to the test.

After the situation with the white boy, as soon as I thought I could relax, my TV blew out. I had the money, but no one to fix it. Craig was gambling heavy at the time, and needed to borrow forty dollars. He asked me for it and I told him no. He insisted he would give it back the following week, but I still said no and told him to get the hell away from me. He walked away cursing and calling me names, so I made up my mind that I wouldn't fuck with him any longer. If that's all he needed to start acting seedy toward me, then fuck 'em.

So for a minute Craig and I fell out.

Well, weeks went by and they called me again to transfer. I wasn't ready to leave. I had ordered a TV and didn't want to leave without it, but I had no choice, so I packed up and said goodbye to Big Lou and the other homeboys... including Craig.

Chapter Seven

They sent me to a place not to far from Jackson called North-side; a real dump located next to a Graveyard. They tried to place me on the 4th gallery but I told the female officer that I was not going up there. I sat there and just looked at her like I was crazy. After a few minutes, three additional officers came over and one of the officers asked what the problem was. She said I wouldn't go to my cell. He asked me what my problem was. I told him I was afraid of heights. He asked if that fact was in my medical file. I politely told him no. He noticed that I had respect for him in the way I talked to him, so he asked her to place me in another cell. She said okay and gave me a cell on the third floor.

When I got to my cell, once again after I turned on the lights bugs were everywhere. This time however I even had bird crap slapped all over my windows. As I stood watching the bird shit, the events that had led me to prison began to play across my mind.

This dude had been tormenting my sister and so I'd taken it upon myself to do something about it. It was my intention to simply pistol whip the guy, but one thing lead to another and I ended up shooting him. The guy died and as a result I was charged with second degree murder. I thought at best it should have been manslaughter, however here I was in prison looking at a possible 30 year prison sentence. As a child, never in my wildest imagination would I have thought I would grow up to be a murderer. A prisoner of the State. Yet here I was standing in the middle of this filthy disgusting cell with no place to sit but on a dirty humiliating mattress.

The next morning I ate breakfast and then went back to my cell to wait on eight o'clock yard. As I waited something told me to ask a guy who was walking past my cell what time morning yard was. He said there was no morning yard so without any other information to go on, for the time being I flopped back on my bed and waited for the guards to inform me of when I could get my property. After about an hour of waiting the officers called yard. I jumped up and headed outside. When I got to the yard, I looked around to see if I knew anybody. A lot of guys knew me, but I didn't know one person so I went to the phone and called my family and gave them my new address.

At this prison, unless you had a job or were in school, you were locked up for half the day. For two months I was confined to my cell with no TV. To occupy my time I read anything I could get my hands on. I signed up for the library, just to get out of my cell. I read a lot of Harold Robins and Sidney Sheldon novels. After a few months, I was placed back in school and given a job as a porter mopping floors.

Even though my mind should have been on attaining my GED, I was more eager to go outside and play basketball or just waste time with the other inmates. I thought taking the GED would take up too much of my time so I ignored studying for it.

During the evening yard, we had the option to either stay outside or go to the gym. The gym had a pool table, card tables, games, and a weight pit. I loved basketball though so I stayed outside much of the time.

Well some months went by and I met a couple of new guys. One of them was D. Moore, he was a neat freak. When I first met him, I thought he was gay. He had a high top fade, slim build, and smooth clean dark skin. Everything with him had to be perfect. On top of that he was a Christian. Guys would tease him all the time because they thought he was gay. We would have some deep conversations and he would cry about missing his wife and son a lot. I never really got into the crimes that the people I met were accused of. To me, I didn't see the point. The bottom line was we were all locked up and that was all that mattered.

I only stayed in this prison for a few months. I got into it with the staff over them basically being assholes. I ended up filing a grievance and they ended up shipping me out of that place quick, fast, and in a hurry. By this time I had turned into a sort of jail house lawyer and these officers had no intention of dealing with my complaints. They were use to treating people like dogs without being challenged so as far as they were concerned I didn't fit in.

I didn't know where I was going next, this time they didn't even tell me. I was simply cuffed and put on the bus. I ended up at I.T.F., a temporary prison. This prison resembled an oversized horse stable, only instead of horses there were men. It was very different from prisons I had been to in the past. Six men slept in one area called a cube. I was used to being in my own cell. Everything was different here; I was use to level-4 and level-3 prisons for guys in trouble and out of control. At this prison inmates were allowed to walk around with very little supervision. There was a ping-pong table, a pool table, a big color TV and a microwave oven in each unit.

I know a lot of you reading this are beginning to wonder what next. Where the hell would I go next. My answer to you is if you like to commit crimes, I only hope that you don't have to go through half of what I did. At this point I had a long way to go.

When I got to this prison I was informed that this was only a level two prison and I was therefore given a chance to see how I could adapt to this environment. The officer who talked to me told me that I was being placed in the first observation cube so I could be watched. In total there were four whites and two blacks in the cube. When I got there I climbed to a top bunk and looked around. There was absolutely no privacy. This place was too open. Anyone could come in your cube and take anything and it was not smart to fight with anyone because he could come back and just walk in your cube and crack your head at any given moment. I would have rather been in Jackson than this place. At least you could feel safe once those bars closed shut.

It was at this place that I finally began to at least consider taking my G.E.D. As part of school though I thought I would also be allowed to take typing which I began to see as an essential tool for writing, however when school began this place didn't have typing. As a result I really couldn't get totally focused on school because my heart was on learning to type more so than anything else so I dropped out.

Compared to the higher level prisons, this prison gave me a chance to rise up quick. It wasn't nearly as big as the other places and most of the people there were non-violent criminals and weren't as tough as they acted. I was definitely out of place because I could back up anything I said. To make a long story short, during my brief stay at this place, I ended up knocking a guy out, breaking my hand in the process and gaining a reputation as a no nonsense hard core criminal. I gave the officers hell with my smart ass approach to the rules and like the last prison was quickly shipped out again. This time however, to the infamous Adrian Correctional Facility.

Me and my brother Fabb

Macomb – 1994.
Malone El, Getti, Sco, Al, Minute Man,
Spencer Holloway, Long, and B-El..

L.T.F.1990.   Me, Fab, and Bubba..

88

1990. Moms, me, and my sister Dee.

1998. Last picture with my Moms.

My sister Dee, me, and my brother-in-law Man-Man.

MCF–1988.   Me and Ray.

90

Kinross – 1993. C.C., Long, Gene, and Score.

Adrian–1990. Four, Kent, me, and Dee,

Chapter Eight

The one good thing about Adrian was that is was only a one hour drive from Detroit. When I got there, I was put in D-unit and bunked over a white lifer named Slim. Regardless of the color of a man's skin, it's hard to face the reality that a man has life in prison. Bunking with this guy got me to thinking about getting my life in order. With all the fighting I'd been doing and my nonchalant attitude about prison, I realized that I could very well do something dumb that could get me locked up for life.

This place was just like I.T.F. except some minor things, like the pool table was smaller and the chow food was different. Every prison is run differently but has the same policy and laws.

Once again I was in an open setting. Again all you heard was guys farting, snoring, talking, crying, and arguing. To add to the punishment all you smell is feet, ass, and musk. And of course the sounds of men getting raped from time to time. For the most part it happens to white boys. White boys are pretty and attractive to black men who like men because of their blue eyes, long hair, clean face and timid attitude. There are some men who willingly have sex with inmates, but of course those are the ones who live and die as well as think with their dicks.

Going to a new prison is like moving into a new

neighborhood. Everybody there knows you are new and wants to get to know you. Most black men come to prison and immediately try to fit in. They try to belong to a certain click. When you come in with a clickish attitude the old timers see you as a product of the system and write you off as a follower.

At Adrian, I started another prison store. This was my means of income to keep from depending on my family. While in prison, we must still live and meet our needs. We must have soap, shampoo, deodorant, toothpaste and food. People think that inmates live well without any expenses. That's not true. In prison there is a lot of food served that is not fit to eat. Sometimes the food is not done or not seasoned properly. Inmates cook the food and may even drop it on the floor from time to time. And to top it off, you are only given child sized servings. All the food that is left over, because they always cook too much, they much rather throw in the garbage instead of letting the inmates get full.

Anyway, my whole day consisted of going to school from eight in the morning to twelve noon, and work from two in the afternoon to ten at night. The rest of the time I played basketball and talked with friends about the streets.

To back up what I'd said about getting life in prison, one of the most respected men at Adrian, a guy by the name of B. T., had gotten life after getting to prison while just a young man fresh in the prison system. He'd gotten into a fight with somebody and ended up killing him. Now he was doing life. This guy was the most humble person that you could ever meet in your life. Everybody use to stop to talk to him and get advice. He wasn't mean, didn't play mind guys, but was just cool. I'm telling you I was beginning to see the light. I began to spend more and more time in the prison library. I found out that the guy from the sitcom 'Rock', Charles Dutton, had done time in prison. That really affected me how he'd turned his life around. I then found out that boxing promoter Don King, author Nathan McCall, as well as author Walter Mosley in addition to others had gotten out and done positive things in their community. I even found out that in some prisons they even let prisoners obtain college degrees. They don't do it in Michigan but it was inspiring just knowing that fact nonetheless. The only thing that Michigan prisons have to offer is a G.E.D. After that, you are just doing time.

I stayed in the library as much as possible. My whole conversation began to change. I began to realize the importance of an education. People even began to see me as a man on a mission. I read many aspiring stories. Like the black heart surgeon whose mother didn't let him watch television as a child, and how that helped him to focus on books and therefore later succeed in life.

I changed my thoughts, my friends, and my environment. I was doing well and staying out of trouble. And then one day, just like that, once again my favorite three headed monster, the correctional officer once again razed its ugly head.

One day as I was going about my business, I was called to take a urine test. They only gave me one hour in which to take the test so I got nervous and began to drink a lot of water because if you get to the clinic and can't urinate then that's the same thing as being found guilty of substance abuse. Wouldn't you know it I got there and couldn't urinate. For that I received a major ticket. I didn't even smoke yet I was given a ticket. After I got the ticket, I went into a negative state of mind. I played silent thinking I was hurting the system. There was a male officer who was very popular with the other inmates, but I never even spoke to him.

Soon after this incident I went to use the bathroom and some guys were in there smoking. While using the bathroom, a guard came in and out of everybody in there asked for my identification. This time I received a ticket for smoking. The officer wrote that he'd seen me smoking and therefore it was his word against mine.

Prison can start making you feel schizophrenic at times. Making you wonder if maybe you did do some of the things you were accused of. Almost the only sure fire way to stay out of trouble was to stay in my cell and remember I even got in trouble in my cell for the soap throwing incident. For the substance abuse ticket I actually lost time and had my date to go home pushed back.

Everything in prison seems to set you up for failure. If a man stays out of trouble for his whole term, the system says he's a con man and knows how to trick the system. If a man pursues his education and attempts to change his life then he has to worry about false allegations and the like.

Prison staff wants full submission of your mind, body and soul. They want you to depend on them and accept whatever they do even if they're wrong.

When I went to see my counselor about the ticket for smoking, I explained to the counselor that I didn't smoke, I hadn't had a ticket in over eight months, that I was in school and doing well. In response he told me I had three days top lock. I asked him how could that be and he said that since I hadn't been speaking to him or any of the officers that I shouldn't try talking to him now and to go back to my cell. So I had to stay locked in my cell for three days.

My friends at this prison were younger guys. There names were J.W. and D.B. J.W. was from the east side. He was a real neat dresser with a very light complexion and good hair. D.B. was a slim dark skinned brother from the Dexter area, which was on the west side. He made sure his hair was cut every two days. They were both well groomed brothers who had a lot of pride in themselves. They also both looked up to me and had a lot of respect for me.

This was J.W.'s first time in prison, but D.B. had been in and out of prison at a young age. He was a product of his brother who was a member of Y.B.I. Every day we would all hang out and play basketball together. When you saw one of us you saw all three.

The only problem with them was their other choice of friends. A lot of their friends would try and get close to me because of the fun they would see us having. J.W. had a friend who was a rat who had told on some guys and everybody knew it. I told J.W. this but he didn't believe me and thought I just didn't like the guy.

About a month later a guy rode in who also knew J.W.'s friend and told J.W. he was a rat. He came to me like a son with his head down and said I was right about his friend. He asked me how I knew. I told him that a lot of guys respected me in prison, and had given me the information out of respect. So J.W. left the guy alone.

D.B. was my man and I learned a lot from him. He was very independent; he wouldn't call his family for anything. He had a couple of girlfriends who took care of him. D.B. had a friend name T.B. who was young and puzzled mentally. T.B. was from the east side and we knew a lot of the same people. I didn't like him because he tried to play both sides of the fence. He would be cool with us and then want to go along with his religious friends. When J.W., D.B., T.B. and I all walked the yard, the gay boys would always stop T.B. They would play in his hair and hold him up by talking nasty and trying to get to know us. I told D.B. that T.B. was fucking those gay boys. D.B. got mad and said he was just cool with them and it didn't mean anything. That a person could be cool with gay people without being gay. I agreed to get along but I just couldn't understand all the touchy feely shit. I wasn't with that at all.

I had to admit that we really had a good time together. We would eat microwave chicken and boxed macaroni with honey biscuits, and drink Kool-Aid to chase it down. I didn't have any habits; I didn't smoke cigarettes, I didn't get high, I didn't gamble, so I was in a position to eat good and have things. A lot of guys got high, smoked cigarettes, and gambled all day. They wouldn't have money for anything else at times and preferred to ask me for things every time they got broke. I didn't give it to them because my thing was if they didn't smoke, gamble or get high, they would have money for basic needs.

In prison I'd heard about female officers and prisoners getting it on, however I had never seen it first hand until I arrived at this prison. One day I was in a cube with a Moe, his name was W.B. W.B. was a good guy and we got along really well. We would play chess on occasion and talk. W.B. was from Saginaw, a small city not too far from Detroit. There was a female officer at the prison that liked him and whenever we would get together he would tell me how much fun he'd had with her. I ran a prison store at the time and she would come down and tell W.B. to get her some Little Debbie cakes from me then she would sit for awhile and then go back to work.

One evening during dinner, I'd decided not to go and stayed down in my cube. I'd fallen asleep and although I didn't know it, W.B. had stayed back as well. All of a sudden I heard a ladies voice tell somebody to hurry up so I lay and played sleep but come to find out it was W.B. and the female guard. I was surprised because she was moaning loud as if she was at home or in some hotel room. As she was leaving, she turned and said that she knew I wasn't sleep and I'd better not tell anybody. I came from under the sheet and W.B. was smiling like he'd won the lottery. He told me not to tell anybody and I said okay.

I wanted to tell my mellows, D.B. and J.W. about W.B. But I didn't know how they would take it. Rumors could get you hurt in prison so I decided to keep it to myself.

A few months later a gay boy came to our unit. D.B., J.W., T.B. and myself were in the same unit. The gay boy's nickname was Lisa, his last name was Day. He was very slim, high yellow and had long hair. Within a few weeks the suspicions I had about T.B. began to surface. T.B. was on this guy like glue. It wasn't long before rumors began to spread that Lisa was T.B.'s woman. Of course T.B. denied it.

Then one day, as me and D.B. was walking the yard, D.B. broke out and said that T.B. was a real hoe! That he was in fact gay. I didn't say anything, I just listened. However after that I never spoke to T.B. again. Whenever he would come around I would leave.

Lisa was starting to get very comfortable with the surroundings and so he also started a prison store. One day he asked me if I had some BBQ chips in my store so I went and got the chips and then handed them to Lisa. T.B. saw that and you could tell he didn't like it. He was very jealous. Everything Lisa did, T.B. wanted to know about it. T.B. even got moved to the same cube as Lisa to watch him. Everybody noticed the change in T.B. He was in love with Lisa. T.B. insisted that he only wanted Lisa's money because his family sent him hundreds. Lisa would buy him things and he would tell everybody his girl bought them. He would follow the gay boy everywhere, even to the shower and toilet. Even Lisa was getting fed up with T.B. I mean this guy was smothering this dude. When Lisa broke away and started hanging around with other gay boys T.B. literally went crazy.

One night, T.B. and Lisa were arguing and Lisa told him that she should be able to see other men.. T.B. got really mad and he hit Lisa in the face. Lisa hit T.B. back and the fight was on. The officers didn't know what was going on and if they did most officers could care less until it posed a problem for them. A few weeks after the fight, T.B. moved to another cube and tried to hang with D.B. again. That was dead!

The female officer who was fucking W.B. was now giving him money, buying him clothes, and taking care of him. Then one day W.B. found out that she was also fucking another inmate. He was hurt. One day we were playing chess and she came down and asked to see him alone. He said no and she didn't like that. She said it was important and demanded he come to her office. He waited a few minutes then went to see what she wanted. When I walked passed her office, she was crying. I was amazed, and then he kicked her door shut and went huffing and puffing back to his cube. When he came back to the cube, he said he had been transferred. He went on to say that she was just a hooker, a freak, and he couldn't let her hold him up. As it turned out though, she really was a freak. Word soon got around that W.B. and the other guy were not the only people she was having sex with.

Meanwhile, T.B. found out that Lisa was having sex with

another man. When he ran into Lisa he demanded that Lisa come to his cube and talk to him, but Lisa said no and walked away. T.B. walked away mad, however, about a half hour after that T.B. tracked Lisa down, grabbed him and walked Lisa to Lisa's cube. There they began to argue and T.B. knocked Lisa to the floor. Lisa tried to fight, but couldn't so some guys broke it up and T.B. went back to his cube. Lisa then followed him to his cube and when he turned around Lisa dug his nails into his face. Blood was everywhere. Lisa then hit him in the face with a huge radio and when he fell to one knee spit in his face, called him a hoe and walked away. T.B. got beat up by a sissy!

It was now November of 1992 and I was being transferred out again. My mellows, J.W., D.B., and I all ate that night in honor of our last night together. We had two boxes of chicken, 3 cups of soup, nachos, pickles and peppers, with hot sauce and BBQ sauce. For dessert we had about 10 honey buns and apple pie. We sat at the table in the card room and had a ball. When you get close to some guys in prison, you don't want to leave them. I grew up without a father and my brother passed away when I was fourteen. To find some true friends that I could love and trust like brothers was a good feeling.

Before I left, I gave both of them all the stuff in my store: chips, cookies, coffee, tea and all the credit of the guys who owed me money. About $150.00 each. I left that place with about $500.00.

That night, I couldn't sleep knowing that I was about to be 10 minutes from my home. I could see my family, old friends, and be around black officers, who I expected to treat me better and understand my situation.

Chapter Nine

The next morning, I got up and everybody in my unit was saying their last good-byes. D.B. playfully punched me and asked me why I had to leave. J.W. and I passed the time waiting shooting pool. He always wanted to beat me and admired my skills on the pool table.

Early that afternoon as I was warming my chicken they called my name to get on the bus. I ate about 2 pieces then an officer came up and gave me my pass to the Control Center. J.W. and D.B. walked me to the Control Center while many of the other inmates yelled their final goodbyes through the windows. When we reached my stop, J.W. hugged me tight and told me to write him as soon as I got settled in. Then my boy D.B. hugged me and told me he loved me like a brother. I told both of them I loved them and would write soon. I then walked into the Control Center and waited with the other inmates. The officer asked us to undress so he could check us and after that we were handcuffed and herded onto the bus. The officer who called us knew me from Ionia and M.R. and referred to me as bad ass. I told him I'd changed but you could tell by his expression that he didn't believe me.

When I boarded the bus, I looked up and saw six guys that I knew from the county jail as well as M.R. It was like a reunion of old friends and I was fit for the party. I had on a pair of gold framed glasses, my clothes were clean and neat, and my shoes were spit shined to a tee. Even with the state clothes on I looked good. I sat next to King Pin, who'd locked down the hall from me at M.R. As soon as I sat down everybody began asking me if I'd seen certain guys who we all knew. Then one guy broke out and said he'd heard about me breaking that guy's jaw at I.T.F. I looked back and it was my dog Fats, a homeboy from the east side. I asked him how he had heard about that and he said a guy we both knew named P.Y. had told him.

As we headed to our new home, everybody occupied the time talking and telling stories, trying to make their story more important and tougher than the next guys.

After awhile one of the homeboys asked the officer for the piss bottle. The officer told him to wait until the bus stopped and mellow told him that he wouldn't need it by the time the bus stopped. Guys started cursing at the officer, telling him to get the bottle but he ignored them. Finally the guy took out his dick and pissed on the floor. It rolled right passed everybody right to the front of the bus where the driver and shot gun rider was. The officer looked down and asked what was going on. Another guy shouted that we'd asked for the piss bottle… The officer then asked who did it. Everybody went silent and started looking out the window. He warned us that we would pay for our actions, but we didn't think anything of it, we just started laughing and teasing the officers.

When the bus hit Eight Mile road going east, everybody went to the windows and began yelling that they were back in the hood. It had been six long years since I'd been in Detroit and from my vantage point, it really looked bad. Houses were torn down, stores were closed and people, at least where we were was pushing store carts filled with black garbage bags. On the flip side we had a chance to really get crazy. Every time a car with beautiful girls would ride by, the bus would erupt. Guys were yelling to stop the bus and let them out so they could go home with the girls. When we passed my old school, Pershing high, it was then that I realized I was in fact in my old neighborhood but would not be going home.

At about 5:30 p.m. we arrived at the Ryan Correctional facility. As soon as we pulled up I immediately saw that things would be different. Fine black women were everywhere. This was definitely going to be a different experience.

I was put in a room with an old black man that smoked. He was from the east side and had been in prison twice for manslaughter. You always get along with your Bunkie during the first few days so in addition to smoking it would be awhile before I found out if we would get along. This would also be my first experience of sleeping in a room with a guy.

One good thing that happened when I arrived was that the same day that I rode in my family came to visit. It was good to hear the latest news about my family and friends. It also felt good to know people cared enough to endure the unnecessary wait and search procedures to see you. My mother would wait no matter how long they made her sit before seeing me.

After my visit, we were called to dinner. During the first

day, everybody goes to dinner hoping to see a friend, homeboy, mellow, or somebody. When we arrived at the chow hall, female workers were everywhere. For me, that alone was a blessing. The first person I saw as I scanned the room was my homeboy K.B. After three long years there he was. My main man. I went to sit by him but a female officer stopped me and said I had to sit at another table. I looked at her like she was crazy because all the other inmates had sat where ever they wanted. So K.B. asked where I'd been assigned and I told him. He then told me he would send me some things as soon as dinner was over.

A few minutes later a lady I knew from the hood walked up and said hello. I spoke back and she told me that she had called my mom and told her I was there. I was really out done because I had wondered how they'd known I was at Ryan.

The guys at the table were shocked to see that she knew me so well. Before she left the table she asked where I stayed then said she would stop by and see me before she went home. W.X. asked me did I know her. I told him yeah, she used to stay in my neighborhood when I was younger. That she use to go with my homeboy Angelo. Then someone asked if I meant the dope man Angelo who'd been killed a while back and I said yes. At that point I felt like the guys were getting a bit too nosy so I changed the topic.

Later that day, as she'd promised, officer B.B. came by my room. The old man, Mr. Moore was there when she arrived, and the first thing she did was speak to him. He looked surprised that she'd spoken to him but spoke back nonetheless. She then looked over at me and asked if I wanted her to tell my mother anything. I told her to tell my mom to send my jewelry. She said she would and then turned and left.

The next day we still hadn't gotten our property and I for one was starting to get a bit antsy. We didn't have toothpaste, a toothbrush, soap, or a change of clothes. All day the guys kept asking the officer on duty to call about our property. Come to find out, because of the piss on the floor incident, the bus driver had taken our property back up north. We didn't get our property back for another week.

A lot of the guys got mad and said they were going to sue the department of corrections. According to department of correction policy, an inmate is supposed to get their property within 24 hours of his arrival to any prison. To say the least however, this was just one of many examples where correctional officers pretty much did what the fuck they wanted.

I didn't really have it that bad because as promised K.B. had brought me a bag filled with everything I needed.

K.B. also took the opportunity to get on me for not having taken my G.E.D. He understood the necessity and importance of it. As a matter of fact he was so disappointed that I hadn't taken it that when I told him he simply turned and walked away. He didn't speak to me again for almost another week.

During my first week at Ryan I also ran into a good friend from my projects named D.R. He asked if I needed anything and I told him a television. At that point he offered to loan me his for a few days. The only stipulation was that he needed it back on the weekend so he could watch sports.

Later that night, when my Bunkie awoke and discovered I had a television, he asked if I'd gotten my property and I told him no. I told him they'd taken it up north as punishment and that I had borrowed the television from a friend.

The next day the old man went right to the officer on duty and for no reason other than ignorance, told her that I had a television in the room.

Well, I don't have to tell you how long that relationship lasted.

After a couple of weeks had passed and I'd still not gotten my jewelry, I tracked down B.B. and asked her when she was going to bring it. Again, she said that she would.

After a few months went by and B.B. still hadn't brought it, I pretty much all but gave up that she ever would. It was also about this time that I began looking for another room mate. Not long after making the decision to move I was transferred to the room of a weight lifter named Big K.

Big K. and I got along for about a month. I wasn't an angel but I was considerate and wasn't a bad person to live with. However, Big K woke up every morning at five o'clock and flicked on the lights. He would either read muscle fitness magazines or look in one of his 20 mirrors. He also went to bed early. On the flip side, I would run in and out of the room until midnight getting cookies and chips because I ran a prison store.

Every thing came to a head one day when I walked in on Big

K shaving his pubic hair. What made it so bad was that when I walked in he was standing in the room naked. Disgusted and embarrassed, I turned around and walked away. Usually when an inmate needs the room to himself he'll cover the window with a towel. As I walked away, I was burning mad. I could deal with roommates as long as they didn't steal, snore, use drugs, or masturbate in the room while I was in it.

When I got back to the room, Big K told me he didn't know I would get back so soon. I jumped off my bunk and told him he should have gone to the bathroom or just put the towel up. Then I told him that he obviously considered the room solely his so I was going to let him have it and move down the hall. He apologized and told me that I didn't have to move, but I told him it was for the best because he went to bed to early anyhow and that could never work.

After about three months of being at Ryan, my sister finally brought my jewelry.

You know, the thing that bothered me most about black prison employees is that you would think that with every thing that we have gone through in this country that black people would not want anything to do with anything that have to do with being locked up. But many of us can't wait to put other people down.

When B.B. saw me with my chain and ring, she had a fit. Any time she would see me after that she would act like she had an attitude. So my attitude was fuck her. At that point I didn't know why she never got my jewelry and I didn't care.

As far as I was concerned B.B. was a fake. She would always have four or five inmates around her, laughing, talking nasty, and dancing. It made me want to throw up just watching her. Then the following day she would come to work and want to play the real hardcore officer. She expected me to be in her face all day but I had learned. The rules from Jackson still applied. Never kick it with the officers.

A few weeks after this episode, B.B. showed up in the visiting room with my mother. When I got there she was crying to my mother about me ignoring her. I waited until she had finished talking and after she left I walked over to my mother and gave her a big hug. Before I could start talking about anything, she asked what I had done to B.B. I explained to my mom how B.B. wanted me to give her attention, but I couldn't because she was an officer and I was an inmate. My mom understood and told me to be careful. That I may have been right but it wasn't good getting any officer upset. She also said B.B. thought I was angry because she hadn't brought my jewelry. But, I wasn't mad about that, I was mad that she kept saying she was going to bring it yet never did.

When I got back to my unit, B.B. asked if I had a good visit. I simply smiled and walked away.

My new roommate and I, a Muslim guy name Noah, got along well. This was my third room mate in as many months and a lot of guys started questioning me about moving so much. At first I tried to explain myself and gave reasons as to why I moved, but then I decided that it really wasn't any of their business. This was my life and I didn't need anybody telling me how to be happy.

Around about this time, I met a beautiful young woman named Doris. She and one of her friends, a young lady named Coco had come to visit my home boy W.X.

I'd seen Doris and Coco around my neighborhood before I got locked up, but I didn't really know them. Anyway, while they were there I ended up having a long conversation with Doris. We both laughed and had a really good time. When she got ready to leave she asked if she could come back and visit. Of course I said yes. It had been a long time since I'd been in a relationship and I was not about to turn that down. On top of that, Doris was fine. She was light skinned, had a beautiful smile, and the prettiest brown eyes. After we met, she would come to the prison every day at 6:30 and stay until closing, that is, until I fucked up.

What happened was, Doris' had a brother named Eric, and Eric was currently dating the girl I was going with when I came into the prison system. Well, one day Doris and her brother were talking and somehow my name came up. Can you believe it? Out of all the people in the world… There I was going back and forth with her about somebody I'd dated almost twelve years earlier. Doris was all I had and the only one showing me love except for my family, but for some reason she couldn't see that. She'd had some bad experiences in the past and because of those had simply assumed that I was like everyone else that had done her wrong.

I did everything within my power to assure her how much I loved her. Then out of the clear blue, Mona wrote me and sent pictures of her self along with her phone number. Well to say the least I was glad to here from her and I called her. We ended up talking for over an hour. I told her that I was currently in love with Doris and she seemed really happy to hear that I was in a relationship. Come to find out, Doris' brother Eric had called Mona and told her that I was at Ryan and that I was going with his sister. Mona then called my family and got the other information.

The following Sunday, Mona showed up at the prison with her little daughter. I was out done. However, because I had used up most of my time with my mother, we didn't have long to talk, so we talked as fast as we could in an attempt to catch up. When she got ready to leave, we hugged and she left. That was it. No kissing, nothing.

The next time I talked to Doris I told her that Mona had come to visit. I felt like it was the right thing to do. But she thought different, very different. She said that I shouldn't have taken the visit and wouldn't let me get a word in edgewise, so I said good bye and that was it. That was the last time I talked to Doris. I wrote and tried to explain my side of the story, but to no avail. It was the end of my relationship with Doris.

Mona came up a few more times but I never told her what happened. She would ask how Doris was and I would simply say okay and leave it at that. That was a lost that really affected me emotionally, because I thought I was doing the right thing.

After that episode, I asked for a transfer out of Ryan. Being close to home was beginning to drive me crazy and on top of that the authorities use to make my mother wait an hour at a time to see me. It was sickening. I wrote a grievance to the Warden about them making her wait and while I was at it asked for a transfer out of there. This time I requested a transfer to Adrian Temporary.

In the process of waiting on my transfer, I earned a certificate of legal research, which pushed me into more positive and productive reading, mainly law.

Ryan was too black for me and too unprofessional. The officers were told that all inmates did was lie, cheat and steal, and couldn't be trusted and that's how they treated us. In fact, it's not like that at all. It's really interesting because when an officer is first employed most are actually afraid of the inmates but once they realize that they are in power, some get out of control. They learn that writing tickets is a form of power and control. The more tickets they write the better. After awhile they're not interested in trying to help rehabilitate inmates just hassle them and give them a hard time.

On top of that I just couldn't jail around my own people, my so-called brothers and sisters, the officers or the inmates. Black people seem to just have it out for anybody that's trying to do anything positive in prison. Of course not all black people do this but in my experience most of us can't stand to see anybody with anything.

Chapter Ten

After a month or so I was called to transfer to Adrian. I made it by the officers with my stamps and was hoping that I could make it into Adrian with them.

When I got on the bus a guy named Louis from Pontiac rode out with me. He was a lifer who didn't give a damn about nothing. He didn't care about the officers or getting a ticket. See he hadn't requested to be ridden out, they just jumped up and put him on the transfer list and he was mad about it. The guy had a bad stuttering problem and he would call them mother and wait about a minute and say fucker. Man that was funny.

Louis was also cursing because Adrian has six-man cubes, which means you have six men to a setting; and on top of that its wide open like a gym. He'd made some enemies and that was not the prime ideal situation to be in. So he kept shouting that he wanted to be locked up behind doors...not out in the open.

When we got to Adrian the first person I saw was the female counselor that I didn't like. She looked at me, made a few smart remarks and I played it off. I told her that I wouldn't be there long so she needn't worry about spending all her energy on hating me. They sent me to the non-smoking B-unit, took my cuffs off and gave me a bed roll. I was shocked because I just knew they were going to make me get naked but they didn't.

Louis came out behind me saying that before the night was over that he was going to be in the hole. He was intent on keeping his word about not being out in the open.

When I got to my unit I was so tired that I lay down and went right to sleep. After I woke up I went to yard and after looking around for a few minutes, ran into this guy I knew from 8 mile named Big Green. Big Green was about six feet nine and weighed well over three hundred pounds. They called him Green because of the color of his eyes. He was with another guy, Gig M-X. M-X was seven feet tall and he too was a big guy. I would later have a few problems with Gig M-X. But for the time being we kicked it and of course I was relieved any time that I ran into people I knew.

My first day went by pretty good. One of my bunkies was a white guy that I knew from another prison and he was real cool. Of course what was so crazy about that first day though was as I was heading to chow, sure enough there was Louis… handcuffed and being led to the hole.

The next day I found out that the white dude in my cube had a female officer bringing him food from the outside. The first time I saw those Wendy's Burgers and Fries was a trip. He had something that I didn't but that was cool. I was happy for him. I only hoped that I could get me a hook up like that.

Right before I left the last prison, one of my boys K.B., had really gotten on me for not having gotten my G.E.D. He'd told me how foolish I was for taking all type of classes except for those leading to my G.E.D., and how when I got out of prison how I would really need my high school diploma. So I really took his talk to heart and began focusing on passing the test. I'd taken it before but I'd only gotten a 44.

When I entered the class, I immediately saw that things would be different than before. The teacher, Mr. Nick was real cool and serious about me getting my G.E.D. Mr. Nick was the kind of teacher who wore a graduation gown and "Nike" gym shoes. He was a real funny type of guy, but effective on teaching the inmates. He saw that I was serious and even had a tutor to help me with my math.

One of the guys in my class with me was M-X. Because of that we began to get real close. He was from the west side and ran with the Pony Down crew. It was all about money with him and I liked that. After awhile me and M-X decided to go into business together. We decided to open a store. He would put up all the money and I would run it. Of course I was excited and ready to make some money. But just like most people who think they can get something for nothing, I turned into more of a sucker than a business partner. In essence I broke one of the rules of prison. Never take something from another prisoner without a total understanding of how that prisoner will get it back.

What happened was M-X invested $55.00 and bought everything that I put on the list. The list had cookies, chips and candy. And I ran the store. See everybody liked and respected me. I was a happy go lucky guy who was very easy to get along with and deal with on a business level. Running a store in prison is not easy because a lot of people are petty. We're dealing with criminals here and a lot of them act just like criminals when it comes to conducting business. They will get stuff from you and then not want to pay you. You know, petty stuff. With me, it was all about profit. I didn't sweat the small stuff. I realized that you would have people trying to get something for nothing but M-X wanted to take things further. He wanted to keep tabs…names. But I had gotten the kitty up to $300.00 so I didn't want to get into all that. I wasn't trying to fight and force people to pay me for a bag of chips if they owed me. We were making too much money. My thing was you just couldn't get any thing else from me, simple as that. I had the whole prison population coming to me to shop, but M-X was becoming very controlling and wanted to keep paperwork and names. It was against policy to even run a store in prison, much less trying to keep paperwork. The reason that we even had to make extra money was that we needed money to buy things like soap, food, deodorant, etc.

If we lived by what the prison gave us, then a lot of men would go crazy.

People had all kinds of hustles where I was. Another guy who shared a cube with me ran the prison basketball and baseball tickets. Like I always say, everybody wants something for nothing, and to bet one stamp to get 20 stamps, a person would definitely take a chance.

After awhile I started seeing M-X becoming jealous of me.

He had a store in all the units, but mine was making more than the rest. I would give him so much, like half of my profits, but he wasn't satisfied, because he wanted full control of me and I wouldn't allow that. I'll be playing basketball... in the heat of the game and he'll want me to stop to go get a guy some cookies, but I would keep playing and when the game was over, I would go get them.

After a period of time I decided to invest my extra money with the guy selling the sports tickets. All I had to do was loan him $100.00 in stamps and I'll make $200.00. M-X heard about me booking tickets and accused me of using his money to do it. Of course I was using my own money, but like I said when people think they got something on you they try and treat you like you're stupid.

I did everything within my power to remain motivated. I even began to dream of getting out of prison and doing big things with my life.

Anyway, one day after the yard closed M-X came over to my unit. He told me that there were some people still in the yard who wanted some chips and other items. Well I went on and got the stuff and while the guard wasn't looking ran out to the yard and delivered the items. When I got back he wanted me to go back again. Going out to the yard after closing time meant trouble, that was a major ticket. So I said no and refused to go. M -X got mad and told me that he'd see me the following morning.

Well the next day about 6:30a.m, he and two of his

Muslim brothers came over to my unit and called me out. I had a feeling about what was about to happen. He told me to just give him all of the stuff from the store and there wouldn't be any problems. I looked at him, smiled and went and got the stuff. I had two guys working for me who had stored stuff in their lockers plus I had about $300.00 worth of stuff. This whole situation ended up bad for me because I tried to make a deal with this guy. I told him that I would have any additional monies owed added to his account but he wasn't trying to here that. He told me that he wanted 10 boxes of cigarettes and then we would be even. Well I had a choice, fight and get into deeper trouble or abide by his demands. I chose to get the cigarettes. A lot of my friends thought that I should have stood up to the guy. Stood my ground, but I was on another level. My focus was on trying to get out of prison. Of course that didn't mean a whole lot to the people who saw me as being soft but I didn't care. I had a mind of my own. I sold a lot of my clothes to get the cigarettes. It wasn't the end of the world because I still had a lot of clothes left. I also lost a lot of friends but hey, I still had the library and I still had my ticket hustle. I got myself into that situation so the way I looked at it was I was probably just lucky to get out of it as easy as I did. It was a lesson learned.

One good thing came out of this period. I took my G.E.D. and passed.

After I finished paying off M-X, I bought me a box of cigarettes, 5 bags of coffee, 10 packs of buglers and opened up another store. In prison coffee and cigarettes are the biggest goods next to drugs.

After I passed the G.E.D., I got even more serious about life. I began to read books by other authors such as Carl S. Taylor, Les Brown and what was to become my favorite book, " Black on Black Violence", by Amos Wilson.

There are a lot of things that I don't like about prison, and don't get me wrong, I know that its not a place for us to like, but I'm pretty much letting people know who may end up there what to expect. But I don't like the fact that when one person does something wrong, everybody gets punished for it. Like when the men escaped from Ryan, every man in prison paid for that, even though all of the men were caught, just the fact that they escaped affected every inmate. They started taking items away from us and we all had to start wearing uniforms instead of our regular clothes.

In prison all inmates are not bad people. When those men escaped there were a lot of men doing life that could have escaped but didn't go anywhere. But they didn't look at that.

Another thing I don't like is how once you've committed a crime and been convicted, it's held over your head for the rest of your life. You could go ten years between crimes and they'll say. See he's a career criminal. It may not be that way at all. Once you've been to prison it's a crime just to associate with another person who's been to prison. A lot is against you once you've been to prison. Of course if a crime is committed in the vicinity of your home, the first person they're going to look at is you. When you go to get a job, especially today, prospective employers can look on the internet to see if you've been to prison.

Now they encourage inmates to get along and stay out of trouble in prison but once they are out of prison, you can't get caught saying hello to another parolee. If we both stay on the same street and both have to go to our probation or parole office we can't ride together. Correction employees don't have any mercy, they don't care. Their whole thing is that this is their job and its not their fault that you're in the system. It's a lot like slavery. People had slaves but their whole thing was that they didn't create slavery so until it was abolished they kept slaves. My whole thing was and still is what kind of people would make this a career. I am not mad at anybody and I don't hate anybody, but as far as I'm concerned if you're not taking the job to truly help, then why are you taking the job. Why are you working in the criminal justice system? I can't see how any black person who has any knowledge of our past as blacks can accept a job in the criminal justice system knowing that they are treating us like less than human. All you here from the guards and other workers is how its not there fault that you got in trouble and so we should stop complaining and do our time.

It's crazy. Instead of giving us seconds during chow, they throw the food away or give it to charities. They give us second hand clothes once a year if we're lucky and the coats they give you are a joke. Try standing on the bus stop in one and you'd freeze to death.

Anyway, I was in this unit for a few more months before trouble hit again, this time I kind of fell into it. It had nothing to do with me. There was this white lady officer who all the guys used to look at and tell how much she looked like a sister. She had a nice body but to me it was nothing like a stacked black woman. But every one kept building her up about how good she looked. Well, this lady would walk up and down the hall, talking to inmates, bending over, shaking her ass back and forth, and then look back to see who was looking.

I had a good friend named J.K. who was like me. He didn't think she was all that attractive and did everything within his power to stay out of her way. One night she was standing in the doorway and guys had to say excuse me to get by. Now instead of her moving, she stood there and two guys got by her with no problem. Then J.K said excuse me three times and she ignored him, so he tried to squeeze by. His arm just nicked her arm, not to hurt her, but to get by her and she jumped like he'd hit her in the eye or something. For that she wrote him a ticket for assault on a staff member. This was a real bold move on the officer's part. The inmate didn't pay her any attention; so this was her way to show him that she was in power.

A lot of inmates come to prison and do their time and try hard to follow the rules and respect the officers. Inmates don't just walk up to the officers and hit them for no reason, because inmates know that any act out of the ordinary may keep them from going home. If you don't bother an inmate they won't bother you. A lot of the problems between officers and inmates are because the officers provoke them. The officers have a job to do, which is to watch the inmates and make sure they follow the rules. But nobody understands that the officer becomes out of control and power struck and will abuse that power when given the opportunity. Especially when they find out that they can get away with it. The inmates are called out of their names, verbally abused, humiliated mentally and treated at times…like dogs. Yeah, we as inmates try to write complaints, but a lot of times that makes it worst, because now you're a target. The officers have friends and before you know it you don't know what's going on. All you know is that you're in the hole for something that you know nothing about.

Now let me make it totally clear that all officers are not like that. Some are fair and handle their job with respect, but they are far and few between.

However getting back to how I got in trouble. Like my friend J.K. who ignored the lady officer but ended up in the hole, I became her next target. Remember, during this time I was running my store and everything was going good. However, one day I walked into my cell and an officer was rambling through my stuff. At the time, like I said, I was selling coffee and cigarettes, the biggest products in prison. This stuff was like dope. I was the man and by me not drinking coffee or smoking cigarettes I was in a position to keep the stuff. The officer noticed me running in and out of the unit so when I left out, he went into my area and did a shake down. A lot of officers are afraid of inmates on direct communication, so they sneak around a lot and wait until the inmate is gone to yard or something. When I came back and saw the officer in my locker, he noticed me and jumped like someone had caught him with his pants down. When I walked in on him he told me to go to the front desk until he was finished. I told him what I sold in case he was looking for something else and he simply yelled for me to go up front. He thought I was selling drugs. He opened all my soap and anything he could check and didn't come up with nothing but one pair of underwear without my name on them. He felt really stupid, but he still felt that he had something. I tried to be honest and tell him the truth, but he insisted that he knew what was going on and he was no fool.

The bottom line was that I was being set up. The lady officer noticed me avoiding her whenever I was around her and one day it finally hit the fan. I worked as a porter and one day I had to ask an officer to open a locker for me and I went out of my way not to ask the lady officer. She noticed me asking someone else and jumped out at me like I had really done something. She checked me for not asking her and I tried to explain my way out of it but she wasn't having it. I knew then that she was out to get me and at that point I started making plans to transfer out of that prison.

I knew it was time for me to leave this prison, so I requested a transfer. One of the few good things about prison is that you get to request a transfer if you're not happy at a particular place. So I picked this place up north called Kinross. A lot of people considered Kinross a racist place occupied by a lot of whites. And it may have been a lil' racist but the good out weighed the bad. I was about sick of my own people around this time so I didn't care. They had good programs up there like building maintenance, welding, plumbing, auto body, and auto mechanics. They had good jobs, a big yard, and good food. It was a place where you could really prepare for the outside world.

That's one of the things missing in the prison system. Some prisons give you certain programs, but they are for prison use only. Like porters, this is a janitor for the prison. But this prison really prepared you for life after incarceration.

While I waited for my transfer to take place I went into a reading mode. It was uplifting for me to read books such as "Mama", by Terry McMillan, and "Black on Black Violence", by a fellow inmate named Amos Wilson. My whole conversation during this time was about good books and people who succeeded in spite of their circumstances. I became very upbeat and positive. There was nothing that could stop me at this point. I was intent now more than ever of making something positive out of my life.

Also during this time, which was 1993, the rapper 2-Pac, who was mostly known for his raunchy lyrics, was rapping about positive issues. His songs, "Part Time Mama," and "Brenda Had a Baby!" also had a huge effect on me. They really hit close to home. I had a child out in the world and had left her mother to raise her all alone and at this point there was nothing that I could do to change that fact.

Well, during my wait to get out of there, no matter how hard I tried, life was not going to be easy. One day I was sitting in the movie room watching a movie and this guy came in ranting and raving about how someone had taken his chair. I had already been sitting in the chair for almost an hour and whether he'd left his ID in the chair or not I felt after all that time that this was a non-issue. But this was prison and nothing is a non- issue. So there I was faced with having to fight or get humiliated by this guy standing in front of me cursing me out. Well with everything going my way at the time, I went on and got up and walked out of the room. Walking out was not easy. My pride was hurt and I could feel everybody's eyes on me as I existed like a dog with his tail tucked under his legs. But I stood my ground. It was so easy to get in trouble at this place and you really had to take a lot sometimes to avoid confrontations.

After about three days of people coming to me and telling me how weak I was about letting this guy run me out of the movie room I broke down. My pride kicked in and I had taken about as much as I could take. My first instinct was to get a lock and bust this guy upside his head, but I thought twice about that move and instead grabbed a State issued shoe with the big heel and headed toward where this guy was. When I spotted him I went berserk. I hit him so many times with that shoe that you'd thought I was crazy. The dude was hollering and yelling but I didn't care. He'd made his bed and now he just had to lie in it. "Smack", went the shoe upside his head, "smack", across his face…"smack", across his back. Finally an old head named Teez snatched me off of him and warned me that the police were coming. I stopped and stood over this fool for a few seconds daring him to make a move. After he didn't, I walked on out the room and headed back to my cube. As I walked out of there I could here this guy yelling about how I'd sneaked him and what he was going to do to me but I didn't care what he was talking about. I'd redeemed myself.

After I got back to my cube the reality of what I had done hit me. I began to get nervous and started thinking about how I would have to watch my back and how long I would have to deal with ducking and dodging this guy and his friends. Of course I wasn't afraid of them, I was afraid of going to the hole, afraid of getting in trouble and getting another ticket for fighting. Like I said before it was hard to avoid trouble and as you can see I hadn't much luck in avoiding it this time.

After a few days, I got lucky. After our mutual friends had gone back and forth about how cool we both were he made the first move. He came up to me and told me that he was sorry about what had happened back in the movie room and that he wanted to make peace. And at that, we shook hands and just like that it was over.

Man what a relief. Remember I was still running my store and I had a lot of stuff. I had like 80 bags of coffee which went for $1.95 a piece, 7 boxes of Pall Malls at $18.95 a piece, 90 packs of Bugler cigarettes at .80 cents a piece and over 500 stamps. I was prison rich and had risked all of that for the sake of my pride.

As luck would have it, a few days after our truce, my transfer came through and I was ready to ship out. The white officer with the big butt who thought she was black came into my cube and looked over my stuff. She asked me why I had so much stuff and I told her that I liked to keep my own stuff because I didn't like asking anybody for anything. It was the last time that I would have to deal with her and I was relieved; even more so when she turned and left me and my property alone. It was a great day.

Chapter Eleven

The next morning at 7a.m., they called me to get on the bus. As I walked to the Control Center, I really made up my mind to continue to change for the better. Usually whenever I would go to the control room and would have to undress, etc, I would complain, but this time I kept my cool. The officer began teasing me about going up north and how cold it would be but I didn't care. As I walked to the bus, wagging like a penguin, chained from hand to foot, I didn't care about nothing that officer had to say. The only thing I cared about was I didn't have to spend another day in that prison.

When I got on the bus, I looked around at the other guys headed for the nine hour trip up north. Like usual you had your people there looking hard as if they had it all under control...shackles and all. There was also a guy on the bus I knew named M-El. He was a guy I knew from the outside who was cool but who I wasn't all that happy to see. He was one of the dudes who'd gotten out once and had promised to keep in touch and after getting out never wrote one letter. He even went so far as to visit my family but yet never once wrote one letter. People don't realize how important communication is to somebody locked up. Especially when you get out and act like you've forgotten all about your fallen comrades. So anyway I ignored him and sat back in my seat and prepared for the uneventful trip up north.

When we finally got to where we were going, the last leg of the trip was the scariest. We were crossing the Mackinaw Bridge and black ice, the most slippery ice of all, was covering the road. As the bus crept across the bridge everyone aboard the bus held their breaths as the bus inched along hoping that we would not fall into the icy river below. It was a horrifying experience.

Finally about 7:30 that evening we arrived at Kenross. An old army base at one time Kenross was huge. I had only heard about the place but I was shocked at the size of the land outside the prison. It was nothing like I'd ever see.

Anyway we pulled up behind the gym and like clockwork several inmates ran out to the bus and retrieved our property. That was something else that was different because as far as I knew only authorized officers were allowed to touch the property of inmates. In my mind, because the inmates had taken our property it seemed like a long time before they called our names to get off the bus. I was anxious because I had so much stuff and I certainly didn't trust inmates with my property. As we walked in the building, inmates were standing around to see if they knew any of us. Somebody called my name but I was so preoccupied with getting my property that I couldn't even focus.

When we got to the desk, the officer was real professional and respectful. He asked us the usual questions which were did we smoke and did we want a ten dollar loan. I said no to both questions. M-El hit me on the side and asked me to get the loan for him but I just looked at him like he was crazy and said nothing. He later asked me why I didn't get the loan for him and I told him. In prison he ran around with a religious group and acted like he was a religious man and as soon as he got out he went right back to robbing and stealing and even when he got money… regardless of how he got it, he didn't send me a dime. So give me a break.

Once we were finished going through orientation, the officer led us to a large gym which had been transformed into cubes. Each cube occupied four bunks with a long table going down the middle of each side. As I walked to my cube, men were at the table playing poker, spades, and chess or just talking. Some of the guys asked me where I'd come from and I told them "Adrian Temp" and I went on about my business of getting organized and wondering where my property was.

At this point it seemed like everything about this prison was professional. They sent us to the chow hall and compared to others it looked like a restaurant. It was big and clean and after we finished eating they sent us to the medical facility where I was given something I'd never been allowed before…a nice comfortable cotton blanket instead of the itchy wool one we were always made to use. The prison even had a none smoking unit which is where I would be staying. I was beginning to like this place already.

As soon as I finished with my medical, I went back to the gym and called my mother. I told her everything had went well and that I was going to really focus on getting myself together. She congratulated me again on getting my G.E.D. and I reassured her that that was only the beginning. As I hung up the phone, I felt real good knowing that my mother knew that I was in a better place. Her knowing that more than anything really made me feel good about being in this new place.

I had come to Kinross to keep my focus directed on my education and I was intent on keeping that promise to myself.

That first night however, was really hard for me because I still hadn't gotten my property. However after tossing and turning throughout the night I was awakened at 4 a.m. by an officer who informed me that I could follow him to pick up my property. Man what a relief. I jumped up and followed him to this small room where my footlocker and duffel bag was located. When I spotted my stuff it was like discovering a pot of gold. Man was I happy. When I got back to my cube I immediately began putting my stuff away, however, in the process the three other men in my cube woke up. In prison, most men judge you on how much stuff you have. They gossip, judge you and base everything on what you possess. To say the least I'd gotten their respect real fast.

I also found out real fast that Kenross had a lot of gay men there and a lot of predators. I noticed that a lot of the gay blacks preferred white boys who possessed feminine traits, with blond hair and blue eyes. They did have rooms at the prison however I had to stay out in the gym for at least 30 days before I would be allowed to get a room. In the mean time, I just had to deal with looking at these guys prance around the gym happy as sissies with a bag of dicks.

At Kenross I immediately put myself on all callouts. I signed up for substance abuse phase one, trucking awareness, the auto body shop, and the library. And in addition to the yard Kenross also had a bowling alley, handball room, racquetball room and showed video movies every weekend. So to say the least, I stayed busy.

After my 30 day wait, I was given a room in the B-unit. Each room held three men where each inmate had his own bed and area. The only thing I didn't like about it was that I was given the middle bunk. I was use to bunk beds or having a room to myself.

I was now in a room with men that I didn't know, but at least I had my own bunk… and my own space. Unfortunately though, this arrangement didn't last long. I ended up getting cool with my roommate Watson and spending a lot time in the room just kicking it and as a result ended up getting accused of making wine. I don't know where it came from that we were making wine but that didn't matter. I was guilty.

The gym was exceptionally loud. From the time that they turned on those bright lights at four in the morning until the lights went out, there was nothing but noise. I can't stand to be accused of something that I didn't do. If an officer ever stopped me for anything, I would tell the truth. Whether he believed me or not I told the truth. I just feel like it's always best to just tell the truth up front, that way you can avoid any surprises.

While in the gym I was still cool with Watson. He remained in the B-Unit but use to visit everyday. I also met another young guy named C.C. who I became real cool with. He was out of Lansing, which is located about an hour or two out of Detroit. We hit it off right away. He had a lot of nice gear like I did and he was also ambitious like I was so we ended up opening a store together. This time everything worked out well and we ended up making a lot of money together.

After being in the gym for awhile, this time I was sent to the C-Unit.

I had been in C-Unit for a short period of time before I got in trouble again. This time for having three sewing needles. For that, they took my radio, and if not for this guard who was pretty cool, I would have ended up in the hole. As luck would have it, about a month later one of my friends got sent home from Adrian and he sent me $250.00 and I was able to buy another radio.

Another friend of mine named Dre-Brown also sent me $250.00 and a winter coat. To say the least, I was a happy fellow right about this time.

At Kenross my reading went to a whole new level. I read Michael Torney's, "Prison and Indeterminate Sentences", I read books by James Baldwin, Richard Wright and Pete Early's, "The Hot House Good Book." I would spend hours in the library. One thing I can say about Kenross is that they give you opportunity. If I would have gone through with my substance abuse class, I could have become a drug counselor. I did go through the first six month segment but I didn't follow through on the second segment. But at least the opportunity was there. Most other places didn't have anything close to opportunities like that.

I stayed at Kinross about seven months with no tickets before I got homesick. During that time I earned three certificates; one in auto body, one in substance abuse and one in trucking awareness. The place was too far for my mother and daughter to visit so with all the good the prison had to offer it couldn't give me my family. So I requested a transfer to Macomb.

Chapter Twelve

After a few months of waiting, I was on my way to Macomb Prison. Michigan has three counties. Macomb, Oakland, and Wayne. Unless you're up in the thumb area of Michigan, most other areas are real easy to get to and not too far. At Kenross I was nine hours away from Detroit. Chicago is four hours closer to Detroit than where I was. So being back close to home was a relief.

After orientation they moved me down to section 28 Top. When I walked into my room this guy was doing push ups so I told him I would come back when he was finished. He said that leaving wouldn't be necessary and got up and introduced himself. Spencer Holloway was a cool good looking cat that kind of reminded you of the singer Tyrese. When we met, he had been in prison for 8 years. An ex member of the gang "Young Boy's Inc.", he'd been there ever since he was about 17 years old. As it turned out, because I was also from the Dexter area where he grew up, we knew a lot of the same people back in Detroit. This guy really turned out to be something special. He was young, confident, and had a life sentence. The man really had an affect on my life because he didn't go about life blaming anybody for his incarceration. He took it like a man. He accepted the fact that he'd committed his crimes and even though he didn't want to be locked up behind bars, he never let it affect his day to day attitude. He remained positive no matter what. He was a true G.

Spense had like 200 music cassette tapes and spent his entire day reading, ordering tapes and looking at ESPN. As Bunkies all we did was read Vibe magazines, check scores and read East Bay catalogs. Every day as I was reading, Spencer would come into the room and tickle my feet. Can you believe it. Life in prison and he's still being funny. He loved to laugh. And he had money. We ate good everyday. Life was so good in fact that the guards thought we were selling drugs. But we weren't. Holloway simply had money. I didn't ask where he got it, but I knew he wasn't selling any drugs. He obviously had saved his money from the outside because as long as I bunked with him, he was never short of funds.

Macomb didn't have a lot to offer in terms of education, except, food tech, so I had to find something to occupy my time. I got a job in the recreation department and while there enrolled in classes on how to officiate hockey and basketball.

I stayed in the room with Spencer for 8 months before trouble came calling. He messed around and got caught with one weed seed in his pocket and in prison, that's major. You'd thought he'd gotten caught with a key of coke. So after that he and I started getting shake downs in the middle of the night for urine test. It didn't matter that I never did anything. The fact that I was in the room was enough. I eventually passed my tests and was cleared, but a lot of rule breaking went on in between that first seed and passing the test on the part of the officers. The bottom line is that once administration wants to do you in, there's not a whole lot you can do about it. Just hope that there's at least one sane person in the bunch. I ended up getting a ticket because I couldn't pee for my first test. It didn't matter that the officer didn't allow me the proper time to replenish my system, I couldn't pee, they claimed I'd held back, and I got a ticket. Simple as that.

After that we started getting shook down every other week. At that point I told Spencer that I was moving. He wanted me to stay because we got along so good but I couldn't take the abuse. He said that it would blow over, but I couldn't wait that long, I had to go!

The staff and the officers gave me hell about moving, so they moved me upstairs with a smoker. We got along well, but he would come in the room smelling like smoke and I didn't like that. So I made plans to move to another unit with my homey Mo-Mo who'd also been transferred to Macomb.

My counselor at the time was a lady named Ms. K. I never spoke to her the whole time I was in her unit. I guess I'd just taken it upon myself to avoid lady officers at all cost. Anyway, one day I had to give her some paperwork so instead of giving it to her this male officer was standing outside her office so I gave it to him to give to her. Man this lady came running out of her office yelling at me like I'd stole something.

"You come back here," she yelled. "You don't send nothing to me by nobody. You wait your turn to see me."

I was actually in shock because I was really on a different

level. Whereas she saw what I was doing as being disrespectful, I'd just had so much bad luck with female guards that I'd just learned to avoid them. But she took it another way. In the end though every thing worked itself out. She checked me about my attitude, I listened and took it like a man and that was that.

Two weeks later Mo-Mo helped me get transferred to unit two. The change of officers was a relief. Before moving in with Mo-Mo he and I would see each other in the yard but we'd never even locked in the same unit. Mo-Mo was cool but the problem was that he was on his way home. I still had 7 years left and now all I heard from this guy was how he was on his way home and how great it would be. On top of all that, Mo-Mo was dating a lady officer, was married and had another woman coming to visit him every week.

After about two months of dealing with Mo-Mo I was moved into a cell with this old dude who was basically a bum. He had no television, no radio and no job. All he did was lay around all day. For the first couple of weeks I would let him look at my television but I got tired of him just sitting there all day and never leaving the room. So I stopped that and only allowed him to watch it when I was in the room. The truth was that I was now in the room with a homeless guy who happened to be in prison and didn't give a fuck about nothing. I tried not to complain and deal with my situation. Guys would visit and he would be in the bed in the middle of the day and we'd try and laugh it off. But after awhile that got old. I stayed in that room for about two months and then got moved again. This time with a young guy named Keymack. Turned out Keymack was a yes man for Mo-Mo so that didn't work.

You might think that I was probably selfish for wanting to move so much, but those of you who have lived with people that you didn't get along with probably understand. Just imagine having to live with a bum who'd spent his who life begging for money then raped somebody and you had to live with him.

During my time in prison, I tried my best to love my own people. In prison, it's mainly blacks against whites so like everybody else that looked like me, I was for my people. But after so many years of the bullshit, it got to a point where I didn't give a fuck about nothing except who was real and who wasn't. If you were white and you proved to be about your business and somebody that could be trusted and treated me right then that was enough for me.

While running my store at Macomb I really began to notice the difference between blacks and whites. When a black man came to my store, he always wanted a deal or wanted to pay a created price for something. Never the real price. When blacks would borrow stuff, they never wanted to pay it back on time. I would always end up getting into arguments over my stuff. After about six months of being at Macomb, I was ready to move again. I know some of you probably think that whenever trouble came that I was always ready to move, but it's no different than living in a neighborhood that you don't like except it's ten times worse and all of the people there are either convicted criminals or crooked police officers. Now tell me you wouldn't be ready to move. Imagine driving down a neighborhood street and the police pull you over and accuse you of doing something that you didn't do, then give you a ticket for doing it, and then when you get to court the judge doesn't want to here anything that you have to say.

Well, that's what we deal with in prison.

In terms of black people and credit. Not all of the blacks were bad when it came to paying debts., however when it's your own people it just hurts that much more.

The whites on the other hand, always paid and when they owed you money, they paid.

When it comes to moving, everybody is different. Some guys will stay at one prison for 10 years. They're called resident prisoners. They accept a lot of bull from the administration, the inmates and the staff, but they deal with this for the sake of family, friends or a certain job.

A resident is a guy who comes to prison and makes it his home. He does things out of context of the regular inmate. Most of the men who turn into residents of the prison turn out to be rats. The officer's love the resident inmates, because the resident feels like he is part of the staff. The bad part about the resident is he wants to be loved by both sides and of course that can't happen. In prison either you're on one side or the other. They also have to deal with wishy washy staff. You might have one group of officers... say on the morning shift that might be all for the resident prisoner but the afternoon officer doesn't give a shit.

Then you have you're political prisoner. That's the prisoner who is really innocent but because of some good prosecutor is spending time in prison for a crime they didn't commit. Now that DNA is big, a lot of these prisoners are now going home.

And finally you have prisoners who committed the crime and are merely doing their time. Some simply got caught up in criminal activities...some are stone criminals and some are neither. Just people who should have known better. Got drunk and killed three people behind the wheel of a car and are now doing 15 years in prison.

There are a lot of people with issues in prison.

Anyway, my next step was camp. I didn't request camp however the department of corrections suggested it but I knew that based on my status, I wasn't supposed to be going there. Simply based on the rules and regulations of the department I knew I wasn't supposed to be going. The reason being that anyone ever arrested before the age of fourteen could never be referred to camp after having committed a felony as an adult. I tried to explain this to the officer but he wouldn't listen. So...off to camp I went.

For the first time in years, I was actually riding on a bus without handcuffs.

On our way to camp, we stopped off at this place called Parole Camp. There we would spend the night. Parole Camp was really a run down apartment building that was so disgusting that it was ridiculous. The closest thing I can compare it to was a burnt out building with the furniture still in it and that's what we slept on.

Chapter Thirteen

The bus on the trip to Camp Casino was full. There were about 30 of us. After having rode on so many buses chained up though, I didn't mind one bit about the crowded atmosphere. When we pulled up to the camp, just like every other prison there were guys waiting to see if they knew any of us. Of course before I could get off the bus people were already calling my name. The first person I ran into was this guy that everybody called Elevator. He was a guy I'd known throughout my years in prison and we were both glad to see each other. They called him Elevator because of his extraordinary leaping abilities. He was a great basketball player headed for the NBA but ended up behind bars.

I was given a room with this big Muslim brother called Heavy. After that I put my stuff up and went immediately to the yard to see if I recognized anybody. When I walked onto the yard I saw my boy Big Cheese. I'd known him from Kinross where we use to spend a lot of time together playing basketball, ping-pong and baseball. He was also from the west side so we had a lot in common. As soon as he saw me he ran over and gave me this big bear hug. He was so happy to see me that he had me wait while he ran to his room. When he got back he handed me a hundred dollars in prison tokens and had a bag full of chips, cookies and other goodies. I immediately took the stuff to my room and put it up. My Bunkie was surprised at the stuff and began questioning me about it and I simply told him that my homeboy had given it to me.

Unlike regular prison, camp has a count every hour. Also you must be up for breakfast by 5a.m. and be at work by 6a.m. or you'd receive a major ticket. It was a really hard adjustment for me. The people were also different. See once you've been locked down in prison for so many years and gotten a chance to see real hard core criminals, ones that they would never even let see a camp, you quickly realize the difference, so it was just irritating dealing with guys who'd never been to a maximum security prison walk around like they were hard.

It was also irritating that whenever I would get into a game, they would call for count. Everything was count. Start reading a book...count. Talking on the phone...count. Count this...count that. I was going count crazy.

Man was it different. The whole psychology was unlike regular prison. Because a lot of guys there were so close to going home, the guards were real quick to give you a ticket. Tickets at the camp were routine. It seemed like if you got in trouble enough times and was sent back to a regular prison that the guards would get some kind of an award or something. Everybody seemed crazy to me. Fights broke out all the time over nothing. People simply trying to prove how tough they were. In regular prison you already know who's tough. When people fought in prison people often died. There were a lot of young guys there and all they wanted to do was fight, argue, gamble, and talk about fast money and quick rich schemes.

Well me, Swan, and Big Cheese ended up being real cool while I was at the camp. Swan had a store and also loaned money. So we became running buddies. Like I said my Bunkie was cool but I ended up bunking with this other guy named Abeya-X. He was in the Nation of Islam. He was a real cool soft spoken guy but the thing that I couldn't deal with about him was the way he jumped whenever someone from his religion asked him to do something. He could be in the dead of sleep and if somebody asked him to get up and do something he wouldn't hesitate. Whatever they told him to do he did.

My whole thing is if you didn't listen to your parents, you didn't listen to your minister; you never listened to anybody and now all of a sudden you're in prison and you're listening to fellow prisoners tell you what to do. You follow every rule and request yet you never listened to your own mother and father. It's just something wrong with that picture so I could never get into the religious thing.

Another thing that happened a lot at camp was people escaped all the time. Mostly white boys with little time. They'd jump the fence at least twice a week and the unique thing about it was it never made the paper. A few blacks escaped from Ryan and they locked down the entire prison. White boys escape twice a week and you never even here about it.

Well, after being at the camp for several months, I'd had enough of that circus. I was ready to be close to home again. This place was way out of my element and it was making me sick to my stomach. I needed to be around grown folk…and once again be close to home.

I told Cheese that I was going to transfer out and it really hurt him that I was leaving. He was up for parole in a few months and even offered to leave me all of his stuff if I didn't leave. He had about six hundred dollars in merchandise but I just couldn't take anymore of that place. I really thought I could go to a better place if I transferred.

I guess looking back I was constantly looking for a better place but in reality I should have just realized that I was in prison. There really was no better place. There are only things that we create in our own minds as being better but once we get to the next place, for one reason or another it really turns out to be as worst as the last. I was living in a maze.

The next place that I went was the Lehman Camp. I went there because they had single rooms. I was really happy about being there because at this point in my life I just wanted to be alone. I was really starting to think that I had found the place for me when after two days of being there, four officers charged into my room with handcuffs. I didn't know what was going on because I hadn't done anything. They threw me against the wall, handcuffed me and treated me like I'd just killed the warden. Come to find out they were handcuffing me because I'd committed a crime before my 14th birthday and I was not supposed to be in camp. Any kind of camp. They considered me a high assault risk prisoner. Can you believe that shit. I was truly fucked up.

Well, while they were processing my paperwork, I was sent to the Kalkaska County Jail. There I was jailed with guys who'd never been to prison and listened to my prison stories like many of you reading this book. It seemed odd to me that they would take me out of a prison setting and send me to a county jail. People with traffic tickets were at the county jail and here I was right there with them. Being there though was actually fun. I spent a lot of my time just telling stories and talking with a lot of guys who were not really criminals and viewed me like some sort of person that they did not want to turn into. It was kinda like one of those documentaries like scared straight. I'm sure after I finished telling the things I knew you didn't have to worry about too many of those guys even getting another traffic ticket.

There was this one guy there that stood out though. His name was Justin. His arms were deformed and he could open a carton of milk and pour kool aid with his feet. For the five days that I was there we became real cool. I wonder what ever happened to that guy.

On the morning that I was set to leave, all the white boys stood in line to shake my hand and give me a hug. In five days I'd made friends like you do when you're five years old when you walk outside and make a friend within two minutes. That five days seemed like a month. I actually had tears in my eyes when I left that place.

My next prison was one located up north called Newberry Dam. Newberry was for guys who hadn't gotten their G.E.D.'s.

It had cubes meant for 20 men per area. In fact there were anywhere from 12 to 36 men per area and on top of that… there was no smoking. No smoking for men where 80% of the inmates had smoking habits. Can you imagine all those people having nicotine fits in one place and they're all criminals. Man, that place was wild.

At Newberry, tobacco was like crack. Guys who smoked would pay $5.00 to smoke one bugler and a paper to roll the bugler was worth 2 stamps. I hated the place before I could settle in good. It seemed like every day I was writing a complaint. I was determined not to be there not even 6 months. This place was off the hook. Gangs, religious fanatics, and men just trying to fit in. Most of them really just kids with grown men bodies.

A six dollar can of buglar tobacco at this place could make you $800.00. Guards would bring it in, prisoners would send it from other prisons, new people would bring it in. Even matches were like gold in this place. If you struck a match and didn't share the light, it could get you killed.

I saw people pay up to five hundred dollars for a can of tobacco.

I didn't know what I had at Newberry. It was a newly opened prison and they needed guys to tutor men and work in the libraries. But my pride got the best of me and I felt like I was being used so I refused to take advantage of the opportunity. I thought I was hurting them by not taking one of their jobs. All I was doing was looking for the wrong in the officers and the prison so I could complain and write them up. My focus was negative and I was blind to my benefits, I only hurt myself. I ended up taking a job as a porter cleaning up the unit. Newberry was super clean and everything was inside. The only time we had to put a coat on was to go to the yard.

The cube I was in was cool. Little Mo Better a homeboy out of the Brewster Projects was there. We slept close together and nobody messed with us. One thing about us project boys is that we stick together. The cubes were wide open and those young boys would steal anything that wasn't nailed down. The 20 man cube I locked in was like a community, somebody was always in there because if everybody left you could forget it.

The craziest thing that I saw at this prison was when this young cat named Ernie arrived at the prison and he began bragging how he had smuggled a large amount of bugler tobacco in. He was acting all cocky like he'd really done something and preparing himself to make a lot of money. The problem was that he wasn't down with anybody and a group of guys hunted him down, stripped off all his clothes and then reached up into his ass and actually snatched the pack of tobacco out of his ass.

If you had bugler or cigarettes, you had better have back up or you could forget it.

Other than the tobacco issue though, Newberry had a lot of good points that other prisons didn't have.

For one it was one of the only prisons up North with B.E.T. (Black Entertainment Television) and light night power on weekends, 12a to 2a. And they had yard until 9p.m. They also had a salad bar for inmates who didn't eat meat and they had a front yard and a back yard.

Like most prisons, it was pretty hard to avoid getting a ticket and this one would prove to be no different. I was there a few months before I got my first one.

Everyday my unit would be called last for chow. And everyday, by the time it was our turn to eat the workers would be rushing and ready to go. Usually red meat was served and because I didn't eat red meat whenever they would serve fish, which they served on this particular day, I would be looking forward to my fish. Well instead of fish they were trying to push peanut butter off on us. I didn't want peanut butter. It didn't matter whether it was extra peanut butter, all the peanut butter you could eat…I didn't want it. I ended up getting into it with an officer about it and to make a long story short ended up getting a ticket. I got my fish though. They had to cook it. But I got it.

I was hot after getting that ticket. My only recourse was to write a grievance complaint on the officer, which was no good. I found out that the officer was going to set me up and say I was in a gang. It was out cold, if you got caught being in a gang they would put you in segregation for 2 years and then you had to spend the next 4 years in level 4. That was a policy for gang members. All of this because I wanted fish. The officer in my cube told me what they were planning for me and that kind of helped me. I thought I was being smart and could go up against the administration. I guess I had begun to read too many books because if I thought I could go up against these people I had another thing coming. So instead of trying to fight, as soon as I saw that officer I immediately apologized. I was lucky I apologized when I did too because he went on an accepted the apology and then took the ticket out of his pocket about me being in a gang and ripped it up. Man that was close.

Right about this time, I got a letter from my boy Cheese. He'd caught an assault on an officer and so was writing from the hole. Because of the assault they'd also postponed his parole. I was fucked up, because I felt if I had stayed until January, then he would have made it home.

What had happened was an officer had attempted to pat him down while he'd had some football tickets on him, and he'd pulled away. For that, he wasn't going home anytime soon. To show you how crazy prison can be, the very next week I walked out onto the yard and who did I see. My dog Cheese. As soon as I saw him, I left the yard and went back to my locker and got him about $25.00 worth of stuff. Cheese was a business man and it wasn't long before he was running a store. He was able to secure a small loan and before you knew it, he along with myself was making big money. Of course we had to hook back up our partnership and just like before we were making money hand over fist. I was making so much money in stamps that I was sending up to $500.00 home in stamps every month. It was against the rules to have over your allotted sum of merchandise, so I'd get rid of my stamps by sending them home to my mother. Cheese used to be obsessed with accumulating wealth and would spread hundred of dollars worth of stamps on his bed and revel in counting them.

We became the talk of the prison among the inmates, however, every other day he would pour thousands of stamps out on the bed and I knew that it was only a matter of time before he got busted.

Well after awhile the officers got wind of him and took about $300.00 worth of store items from him. I was at my limit when they busted him so when they got to me, I was cool.

In February another one of my friends rode into Newberry. His name was Country. We'd spent time together at M.R. and then in 1995 at Macomb. When Country got to the prison, he smuggled in four cans of bugler. I hooked him up with a connection to get rid of it and he gave me a lot of it for myself. Things like that was always fun, but the truth to the matter was I was still in prison. I had learned the tricks of the trade… how to survive etc., but I was still locked up. I'd entered the system at 25 years old and was about to turn 38. When I came to prison I had no plans for the future, no goals, no education and didn't care about nothing.

At this point in my life, I had no real friends, except the ones I had in prison.

I didn't have six people to carry my casket if I died. I only had one number on my phone list, which was my mother's.

Every job I ever had was as a janitor or a porter. It had been my goal to really turn my life around by this point, but I was really just caught up in the system. I began to think more and more about how I'd hurt my family as well as the man I killed family. I started realizing more and more about missing out on my child's upbringing. Deep down inside I knew that I had to start preparing for my release and what I wanted out of life.

I started really noticing my surroundings. They're so many men in prison, who just live and never have a goal to be anything. They're men in prison whose whole day consist of nothing more than watching television, smoking cigarettes, drinking coffee, playing games, and talking about the past. That's it.

The most dangerous man in the world is a man who wants nothing out of life and can't tell you where he wants to be in 5 years. Prison doesn't give people any hope. A lot of black men never reach their full potential or try to achieve anything productive. All they want is fast money and the fame that comes along with it. Many of us can tell you everything you want to know about Michael Jordan but can't tell you anything about ourselves. If he does tell you about himself, thirty percent of it will turn out to be a lie. You have black men in prison today who can play basketball better then Michael Jordan! They can play baseball, chess, ping-pong, run track but their concept of life is totally distorted.

We do things for attention from everybody else, but nothing for ourselves.

To show you how messed up our minds can be, me and Cheese got into it with some guys because I loaned this guy a cassette tape of a movie. When the guy gave it back he'd switched it with one that didn't work. We were actually about to go to war over a tape.

Well once again another transfer had gone through and this time I was on my way back to Kinross. I gave Cheese everything I had. Like the last time, he didn't want me to leave. We shared everything and the trust between us was true. He told me that he'd send me a hundred dollars in a few weeks and that was it. I was once again, on my way.

Kinross was about 3 hours from Newberry and I had big plans when I got there. It's bad when you say one prison is better than another prison and that you would rather be at a certain prison, however I must say that Kinross was the best prison in Michigan. Mainly because of the programs that they had for the inmates, the yard, the food and the way you are treated by the officers. The T.V. station had over 44 channels and they had black movies like "Booty Call," that they would show every week. All the opportunities were at that prison and it was up to you to make your stay positive. Plus they still had the factory where the inmates could make $100.00 or more per month to support himself. You could occupy your whole day with just work and programs.

Chapter Fourteen

When I got to Kinross, I thought I knew what to expect, however they had made a few policy changes. We could only get 15 minutes on the phone and each call was recorded. The cost of the phone calls had went up and it cost $3.00 just to see the nurse and regardless of your problem they gave you ice to fix it.

With everything that's already going on in prison, policy changes really adds to the chaos.

Once again, I started dealing with me and looking into myself. When I got classified, this time I asked to work in the library. I felt bad because I had a chance at Newberry and had passed on it.

After my 30 day orientation in the gym, I was moved to unit B-1-50 with two other men. A Jewish guy and a crack smoking womanizing otherwise successful black guy who they called Deacon Yea. As soon as I got there Deacon Yea started preaching to me about my life and what I needed to do to get out of my situation and make my life better once I got out of prison. He'd been in prison four different times yet was spending all his time and energy trying to tell me how to live my life. I'd made one mistake and here this guy had come and gone four different times. Can you imagine living like this. Always trying to think positive but always having to deal with people like this day after day, month after month and year after year. Man.

Two days after being in the B-unit I was offered a job as a porter. At $24.00 a month that was considered good money in prison.

Meanwhile, the Deacon and the Jewish guy weren't getting along and whenever the Jewish guy would go to sleep, the Deacon would make all the noise he could to keep him awake. And when the Deacon would try and sleep the Jewish man would make all the noise he could to keep him awake. Meanwhile all of this chaos kept me awake. Whenever I would try and talk to the Deacon about this he would try and get me to take his side. He would talk to me, and try and offer me stuff, but I saw right threw his little tricks. Then when the Deacon would leave, the Jewish man would talk about the Deacon. What I didn't understand was that they both had the option to move to another room, but both refused to move. So I just stopped talking to both of them.

I used my daily routine to keep me focused. At 7a.m. I would go to the gym and jump rope or play ping-pong until 8a.m. which was yard time. Then I would go out and run 5 miles. I also began to hang out with guys who were into vitamins. Mainly C and E. Guys who knew what the best shoes were to run in and which books about running were good. Then at 6:30p.m., I would go to a small business class and on Sunday I would go to a Criminal Law Class.

During this time I had actually become a pawn in the

Deacon's games. He would do things like slam the door when he walked in, leave the light on when I tried to sleep or anything to irritate me. But I simply held my ground. I had already asked for a transfer to another room so I was just biding my time. I would be mad as ever, but I wouldn't say anything.

After a few months or so a friend of mind rode in named Rock. Rock had come in from Newberry and told me that Cheese had been sent to the hole again. This time for threatening behavior toward an officer. I was beginning to wonder whether I was good luck for the man. It seemed like every time I left he ended up getting his stuff takin' and being thrown in the hole. Anyway come to find out, Rock's father was the Deacon. Can you believe that shit. I was rooming with a man I hated who happened to be the father of a friend I was cool with.

The way I found out that the Deacon was his father was that I'd walked into the cell one day and had over heard the Deacon talking about his son having just rode into the prison. When I saw Rock the next day, I asked him was the Deacon his father? Turns out Rock had no respect for him because for one, he had never done anything for Rock. And on top of that, Rock knew his father was nothing more than a prison rat. I told him about what his father had done to me and he told me to do what I had to do. Fuck him. When the Deacon found out that I knew his son, he tried to make conversation about him. But I didn't have shit to say to him. I didn't care if that was his son or not, that wasn't going to make me change my attitude about him.

I was trying with all my might to focus on the positive things that life had in store for me. I entered every program possible and did everything within my power to keep to myself and try and focus on getting paroled.

During my time in prison I'd already completed the following courses. They were:

Life role competency 1986

Group Counseling class of 1986

Building Maintenance Technology One 1989

Drug Awareness 1990

Vocational Counseling and Pre Release 1991

Legal Research Class 1992

Tutor Training Class 1992

Stress Reduction Class 1992

G.E.D. 1993

Black African American History 1992

Substance Abuse Awareness 1994

Trucking Awareness Class 1994

Hockey Official Class 1996

Basketball Official 1996

Small Business Class 1997

Criminal Law 1997

Anger Management 1998

Personal Growth & System Adjustment 1999

Psycho Therapy Assault Offender 1999

In my mind I knew that the parole board would look at

everything that I'd accomplished and say that I'd done them just to get paroled. Can you imagine how hard it is to concentrate when you know that's what the authorities are thinking when you're really doing your best to really become a better person. You really have to step outside of yourself and be the strongest person ever and just do what you have to do to make it in spite of what anyone else thinks.

So many things come at you in prison when you're trying to do right that most people would probably break...and many do.

During this same time as I was dealing with the Deacon and trying to move to another room, clear out of the blue, a friend of mine from Adrian got paroled and immediately went on a raping and robbery spree. I actually had pictures of this guy and myself in my room. I was cool with this guy and now he was all over the news as one of the most wanted criminals of the day. What the fuck! When I heard that I rushed to my room and grabbed those pictures and flushed them up under the toilet. I didn't want anything to do with ever having knowing this guy, but it was too late. The next morning I was called over to administration and grilled by two men in suits about my relationship with this guy and did I know his intentions when he got out, etc. You would have thought that I had something to do with this man getting out and doing what he did. I was trying to get out myself. I don't know what possessed him to do what he did. I guess he went crazy or something...how the hell would I know. All I knew was that I had no intentions of doing anything close to that when I got out. I started wondering if what this guy did would come back to haunt me. The officers told me that if they found out that I'd been communicating with the man since he'd gotten out that I would have to answer to them.

Man, I just wanted time to pass so I could get the hell outta this nightmare and go home. So once again, I put in a transfer. This time to Macomb. I felt that I really needed help and the only person who could give it to me was my mother. I needed to be as close to home as possible.

While I was waiting for my transfer a couple of guys I knew from the prison died. One of a heart attack. So now I started getting paranoid about dying. I started wondering if I would die in my sleep and never get another chance at freedom. I started eating right and taking vitamins…as if doing that would somehow save my life. I was 38 and in my mind I didn't know how much time I had. My mind started playing tricks on me and it got to the point where I didn't know whether I was coming or going. I'd never done drugs but I felt high. I never drank alcohol but I felt drunk. Punch drunk. I trusted no one. Nobody could really help me but myself and even I was starting to doubt my own abilities to do that.

So once again, I was ready to ride. However, bad luck struck again. I was trying to go back to Macomb, but when my transfer came through all they had open was Brooks Muskegon which was 3 hours from my family. I may have well stayed at Kinross, but I went on and accepted the transfer to Brooks.

At 4a.m. the next day I was awakened to hit the rode. I gave my Bunkie a hug then was led outside where the frigid cold immediately woke me up. You haven't experienced cold until you've spent time in northern Michigan, especially with those thin State shoes and thin State blue pants with no long johns on at four in the morning.

Because of what had happened at the last Muskegon prison I'd been to, I was somewhat worried if an officer from the last location would be at the new place. Usually it took me going somewhere before I had a problem but this time I just wasn't sure I was making the right decision. After having been to so many places, my mother told me that I should learn to accept where I was and to stop moving so much. That I should just accept one place and learn to deal with the people. But with options I didn't see any reason to do that. It's like having to go into a mental facility and staying six months then having the opportunity to go somewhere else if the people there were driving you crazy. You know the next place is probably not going to be a whole lot better, but you hope that it's somewhat better than the last place.

Chapter Fifteen

When I got to Brooks they put us in a holding cell with six bunks in it. We were supposed to go straight into population so I immediately wrote a complaint about it. The next day I was given a room but I already had a bad feeling about this place. This place was really unorganized. When I went to get my property the property lady had taken my vitamins and they were trying to keep my typewriter. I had to show paperwork in order to get it back. They went through my pictures and started nit picking about them. One of my friends had his hands up in a peace sign jester and they accused me of being a gang member. She let me send a lot of the pictures home, which was all right, but they decided to keep my typewriter.

After about a week I noticed that each shift was running the prison differently. The morning shift, which were all white officers were not too bad. With them it was just follow the rules and respect them and they were happy. But at 2p.m., which was shift change, the black officers would come to work and all hell would break out. They wanted full control of every movement and every last rule was enforced. You would expect the day shift to act the way the night shift acted and vice versa but the blacks treated us worse than the whites.

I attempted to show the different guards my papers for my typewriter on more than one occasion, but this one officer actually accused me of making up the paperwork. I'd had the typewriter for years; all they had to do was confirm this fact with at least 10 of the last prisons I'd gone to but these people wanted to be the Gestapo or something. As I said before, they are trained to think the inmates are always wrong and these people had that attitude bad. I was mentally upset because I knew that I was right and I knew the paperwork was valid. I'd bought the typewriter in 96' and now these people were trying to keep it. I'd been to Newberry and Kinross with it and had paperwork for each prison, but because my prison number was not on the typewriter, then I was being denied it! So I called my mother and asked her to call Brooks and see if they would call these people and tell them that the typewriter belonged to me. Four days later I had my typewriter.

Even after going through all of that the officer tried to act like he was doing me a favor by giving me back my typewriter. Man, some people were really brought up to hate their lives.

My Bunkie here was an older guy. He was real tall and slim and real cool. We got along great except in the mornings. He was a tutor and got up before 6a.m. every morning and when he got up the first thing he did was turn on the television. I'd often asked if he could use his headphones when he got up and he'd say yes but he never did. Then when he'd come in from tutoring he'd want the lights off so he could take a nap so when I was in the room I was also forced to take a nap just to get along.

This prison was really different in a lot of ways. The guards acted like they didn't know anything about department of correction policies except for the ones that benefited them. It seemed like they just made things up as they went along. For example at every prison in Michigan, you are able to take one piece of fruit out of the Chow Hall, in case you got hungry late at night. Here, it was against the rules. You were also only supposed to have one job, here you could have two. It is also Correction policy that no inmate is supposed to supervise another prisoner, but here they had head Porters who were in charge of other Porters. And finally the place was supposed to be a non-smoking facility, yet everybody smoked. They gave inmates tickets for it, but people still smoked.

The prison was made up of guys from all over the State. Muskegon, Grand Rapids, Benton Harbor, Holland and Detroit. But the Muskegon guys felt like they owned the prison, because it was located in their city. As far as I was concerned the officers had helped create this state of discrimination. Probably because the place was small and a lot of officers knew the prisoners from Muskegon.

For example, inmates from Muskegon got to keep there Easy Rider's Motorcycle club books, and their Rolling Stone books which had all kind of tattoos and gang signs in them yet they took away my Vibe magazine. The Rolling Stone and Biker magazines had naked women, men holding beer, fingers up saying fuck you and men and women with tattoos, skull heads and confederated flags. They even had ways to make bombs in those magazines in the general library, yet they took away my Vibe because somebody in the book had a tattoo.

After a few months this guy that I use to see at Newberry named Head came up to me and we started kicking it about life and prisons and the like and come to find out he had a white Bunkie that he didn't want to room with. So we made a deal to become room mates. I'm telling you, the guy was cool but had a head like a sludge hammer.

Come to find out this dude was deranged. Also during this time, a family friend, a pretty young lady by the name of Julia Brown died. She had been a closer friend of my sister's however she would often visit. With the other two deaths and now her, I began to really get paranoid about walking out of prison.

Because I had already taken all of the classes that were being offered at Brooks, I was not allowed to take any classes. The only thing I was allowed to do was work. I was bummed out about that because I felt that I should be able to take the classes over if I wanted to. What could it hurt. I felt it was better than doing nothing. At first they wouldn't even allow me to work. You'd really thought I'd done something to these people. I hadn't done anything. Just tried to live my life but yet I wasn't allowed to get a job for at least three months after I'd gotten to this place.

Anyway I moved in with my new bunkie Head. The first couple of months were cool. We talked, ate together and pretty much hung out on a regular basis. At first he was the perfect room mate. After a few months though, I started noticing his actions and watching him. He turned out to be one of those Black guys who use to be in love with a white woman and because of that somehow thought that he was better than everybody else. He went over board trying to impress people and was always saying one thing, but doing something else. After awhile his true personality really started to come out. I began to notice that whenever he was on his bunk, he would spend most of his time masturbating. Every time I'd walk into the room he'd have his hands in his pants. I'd walk in on him, catch him masturbating, leave out for about an hour and then come back and he'd still be sitting in the chair with his hands in his pants. It got to the point where I couldn't stand him to touch me or be near me. I mean he wouldn't even take a shower, wash his hands or nothing. So I basically just stopped talking to the guy. I started acting like he was a ghost when I was in the room. I simply totally blanked him out. He was just disgusting.

Every night, he would take toilet paper to bed with him, but never blew his nose. The bed would be rocking and he'd be huffing and puffing while I'd lay on the top bunk playing sleep. Eventually this guy, seeing how my attitude was about him tried to flip the script and started going around telling the other inmates that he simply didn't like me and therefore was going to kick my ass as a result. Nevertheless, I maintained my composure and stayed to myself. But that wasn't enough for him. He would leave the T.V. on real loud, leave the light on until 12 midnight and do all he could to get on my nerves. But I held fast and stayed silent. This guy was really stupid.

He never noticed that all the guys he talked to about me didn't like him and would turn around and tell me everything he'd say. And to make matters worse, he held the position of head porter. That must have been a joke because until this day I still haven't gotten the punch line.

Also during this time, one my favorite aunts passed away. Just that quick, two people that I loved dearly had died. It seemed like nothing was going right while I was in this place.

After several months of dealing with Head, I finally got moved to another room. Again with a man doing natural life. He was very cool and we got along great, but he had been in prison 21 years and he would get upset whenever I would talk about going home. So I had to watch what I said around him.

During this time it had been almost three years since I'd seen my mother. Then one day, I got a surprise visit from her. She was only three hours away at the time but that was really a long ride just to visit for an hour or so. She was excited that I was coming up for parole and so we spent a lot of time talking about the parole hearing. Man was I happy to see her. The whole time she was there I just kept gently rubbing her back trying to comfort her and making her feel as good as possible. I wished so much that I would have just thought about the amount of pain I would cause her before committing that crime. I hated that I was a part of the Black on Black violence in my community and what my actions had done to my family as well the victim's family. Seeing my mother always really

169

made me think about my actions and watching her go home without me was always the most painful thing that you could ever imagine. I really loved my mother.

While at this prison I prepared for my first parole hearing. I had been giving 15 to 30 years and technically I could spend up to 30 years behind bars. As preparation for my possible release, I was put into a psychotherapy class. The purpose was to see if I was fit for society. I was really motivated to attend the class but I didn't have a lot of faith in any counselor whose job it was to determine if I was fit to go home. Fortunately I got lucky and got a black psychotherapy counselor who was fair and understood that I was truly working on becoming a better person and not just there because of the possibility of being set free. It would be a year before I would be up for parole, but after spending as much time as I'd had already, I could deal with another year.

While I was in this class, I got moved into a cell with a Christian brother named Curtis. Everybody considered him to be crazy, because he did nothing but pray all day. He had turned Christian while in the county jail awaiting his fate. He use to always say that Jesus was talking to him in his cell. This was his second time in prison. The first time he was in prison he'd been a beast. A real hard guy who didn't take no stuff off of nobody. This time he was just the opposite. Real laid back and humble. He'd even given away his television and radio so he could have more time to read his Bible. Nobody expected us to get along. All I heard was how it wasn't going to work and how crazy I was for moving in with him. But he wasn't a bad Bunkie at all. He was also from the east side and after talking with the guy he was really an okay dude.

The one thing I could say about him, was that he was serious about Jesus. He would pray for hours then get the Holy Ghost and yell and holler to the point where you could hear him all up and down the hall. I would let him have the room from 7 to 8 every night then at about eleven I would get on my knees and pray with him. He liked that. I believed in God, I just didn't follow any prison religion or believe in religion, because I believe it splits people up. I believed in God and God only! I followed God and God only. God is not a God of confusion and to be put in a position to pick and choose something as far as I'm concerned creates nothing but confusion.

Everything was pretty much going fine up until this point. Then on January 3, 1999 the officer in my section came by and told me that I should call home. I knew that something must have been wrong because I had never been told to call home before. I figured that one of my relatives had gotten injured or something but until I actually called I wouldn't know. When I got through to the house a friend of the family named Tracey answered the phone. She spoke and by the sound of her voice I knew something bad had happened. When my mother hadn't answered the phone and then Tracey answered, my whole body went numb. As I waited for my sister to come to the phone I nearly fainted at the thought of what the news might be. Finally when my sister came to the phone she told me that my mother had died. I couldn't believe it. I wanted to just fall to the floor and break down right then and there. My mind was rolling like a fireball headed straight for total destruction. I got off the phone and went to my room and fell out. I hit my knees and prayed and cried harder than I ever had. It was hard to handle a situation like that from prison and not being able to be home with my family was almost more than I could stand.

After about two days I told a few of my friends and the news spread around the compound like wild fire. The compassion and support of my fellow inmates was overwhelming. They brought food, cards, whatever they could to show their love and support. They really saw me threw that painful experience.

Please let me say at this time, that from the bottom of my heart I am sorry to the man's family that I killed for taking their father away from them. I would never wish the pain of death on anyone. Death is a terrible terrible thing.

I was fortunate enough to make it to the wake to view my mother for the last time. The prison charged me eight hundred and ten dollars to take me from Muskegon to the Swanson Funeral home located on the eastside of Detroit. I got lucky and had two all right officers to drive me. When I left to go to prison my daughter was only 4 months old. My baby sister was 4 years old and was now 18. She'd turned into a very pretty young lady. My sister Dee, who was 16 was now 30, and my sister Conya who was 21, was now 36. I also saw my nieces and new nephew Little D. Everybody from my family was there.

As I walked up to the casket, I looked at my mother and dropped to my knees. My head hit the casket and the officers came over and took the ankle cuffs off so I could stand. I just stood there and looked at my mother lying there. Then I kissed her and cried all over her, wishing I could help her, wishing that it would have been me, instead of her.

My biggest regret was that I never got the chance to make her proud.

Before I left to go home, I had a chance to spend time talking with my daughter. It was a beautiful experience. She asked me when I was coming home and I told her I would be home soon. I didn't know if that was the truth, I did have a parole hearing coming up so I could only hope for the best.

My out date was January 1, 2000, at the time it was January 10, 1999 and I had been in prison since 1985.

I stayed another half hour and I gave everybody a hug. My daughter had tears in her eyes and didn't want to let go. When I got back to the car I waved to everybody one last time and that was it.

From that point on my concentration was focused on one thing. Getting out of prison and taking care of my family.

April 02, 1942   January 02, 1999

A Service of Memory Celebrating The Life
-of-

GENEVA JONES

Saturday, January 9, 1999
12:00 p.m.
Brown's Chapel
Detroit, Michigan

Rev. Freeman Brown, Officiating

My mother's brother Uncle Jr., me, and my daughter Kashira

Andre, Ada, my sister Conya, my brother Larry, me, and
my cousin Debbie sitting to the far right

Uncle Jr., Larry, Grand Papa, Uncle Jabo, me, Andre, and Debbie

Uncle Jr., my brother Larry, Sylvester, and Andre

Chapter Sixteen

On the 11th of June of that year, I rode into the Mound Road
Correctional Facility. I was hoping that this would be my last
trip before going home. I had it in my mind that I had to do
everything within my power to insure that I didn't let anything
come between me and that parole board.

As soon as I walked though the door I was given a urine
test. I was awfully nervous about the test and found it hard to
urinate. I had no reason to be nervous. I guess it was just the
accumulation of everything going on in my life.

I moved into a room with a young guy named H.B. H.B.
didn't have a television, a radio or nothin'. Another guy that I'd
known from Newberry and Kinross was in the room next door
and when he saw me he started acting like we were real cool,
but in fact I didn't even like the guy because he was a trouble
maker. He was known for keeping up a bunch of confusion.
As far as I was concerned he took prison as a joke. He was one
of those who just lied for no reason. He even told everybody
that he knew me from the free world and that was a flat out lie.
I'd met him in prison. He wanted to be a prison dog… prison
slick, a wannabe. But he was actually just a regular guy from a
good family that always sent him money.

Me and H.B. ended up staying up until 4 a.m. talking. He
was real cool. A young guy who'd made some mistakes who

was trying to find himself. He was another guy from the east side and he also knew a lot of the same people that I did.

The next morning I went and got my property and when I came back to the unit, there were two black officers in the unit arguing with an inmate. They'd moved me to another room so I was basically going to my room to get what little I had there. They moved me into a room with this Muslim guy with locks. He wasn't there when I first got there, so the police gave me a key and let me in. About a half hour later he walked in. When I turned around to greet him he was already griming me as if I had broken into his room. So I immediately broke the ice. He then asked me if I smoked or snored, both of which I said no to and of course he was cool with that. Turns out the guy wore a hearing aid but he could read lips real good.

When I walked onto the yard I saw so many old faces it felt like a family reunion. There was Dulin-Bey, Getti, Mike Calvin, Donnie B, Big-O, Eric Pratt, Fox, Soloman Bey, Lil Phil, Murray, Big-C and my best Bunkie, Pee Wee. It was a homeboy reunion, I hugged guys all day and it was real good to see them all.

A lot of mellows went and got me food, cookies, chips and candy bars and for the rest of the time we just stood around the yard laughing and talking about people that we'd seen around the State.

As I was leaving the yard I ran into two brothers that I'd started prison with 15 years earlier. I hadn't seen them since and it was real strange seeing them 15 years later. As I went into the unit I had about ten packs of cookies, 5 bags of chips and ten candy bars. The officer stopped me and asked if I was intending on starting a store, but this guy stepped up and told him that I'd just gotten to the prison and that the other prisoners had given it to me so he let me go with the stuff.

The next day, I got a visit from my sister. It was good to see her. She had mixed feelings about me being in the facility because she knew that it was run by blacks and she knew that based on past treatment by blacks in the department of corrections that I wouldn't like it.

The good thing about being at Mound though was I was close to my friends, I had light night power for T.V. and radio, we had video movies on the weekend, Detroit news on T.V. and WJLB on the radio. Also, the police at Mound didn't do a lot of cell checks and didn't shake down rooms all the time like other prisons, so that was cool.

When I got to Mound my feet were really in bad shape. I had heel spurs on both feet and because of the constant pain, it was real hard for me to walk.

The only solution was to cut off the spurs so I was looking forward to taking advantage of the medical facility at Mound

Well so much for that thought. Mound refused to give me the procedure so I continued in pain. I wrote all kinds of complaints about it but it didn't help. Like I said before, just the fact that the facility was run by blacks didn't surprise me that they wouldn't do the procedure.

I knew that in spite of the number of friends I had, that

I did not want to stay at this place but I had no choice. I was shipped here to see the parole board. I didn't know if I would get paroled…in my mind I was expecting to get flopped. Each flop would add another 12 months but I knew I could handle it if I had to. I'd known numerous guys who'd gotten flopped and damn near lost their minds not knowing if and when they would get home.

After 15 years of not being home, I actually considered prison my home. No I didn't want to stay, but 15 years is a long time to be institutionalized. To be programmed into one way of thinking. For example stamps was like money to me. To those of you who've never been to prison that may seem strange to you, but to us, its money. As a matter of fact almost anything of value in prison is the same as money. I hadn't walked down a street, swam in a pool, sat on my front porch or petted a dog in 15 years. For me it would be like a stranger going to a place that I once knew. Like going to a different land where people took advantage of such simple things as privacy. The simple freedoms to make decisions as to what to do on a daily basis without anyone telling you anything different.

But for now, I was still a prisoner. When the time came for me to go before the parole board, I couldn't because my Psychological Report wasn't done so I had to wait an additional two months.

My counselor at the time was this young cat named Mr. Gleason. He was real cool and kept me focused. We use to talk all the time and he was real cool. He was street savvy and didn't act like he was better than me because I happened to be in prison. He used to make me laugh every time we were together. The one important thing was that he respected me and the other inmates as men and he did what he could for anybody.

During this phase of my sentence I passed a lot of time playing ping-pong, jumping rope and going to the gym. I could work out on my foot in the mornings, but after that I was too sore so I stayed in my room for the remainder of the day.

Being at Mound was cool in some ways and like I said irritating in other ways. It was only 20 minutes from my home, but you know the funny thing was a lot of people who were supposed to be my friends never came to visit. To some degree, I could understand, because the prison staff treated everybody that visited like prisoners themselves. Everybody had to take off their shoes, get patted down and if you had false teeth you even had to take out your dentures. So in that way I understood. But I still felt like I'd been left on some deserted island and nobody knew how to find me. I tell you, I have nothing but respect for the many women who visit prisons. Thank God for making you strong enough to understand. Trust me, I understand it's not easy.

I was now weeks from seeing the Parole Board and I was worried. I was looking for a 12-month flop; just because of my past history and past prison record. So my mind was made up. I wanted to get out but I didn't think it would happen.

Finally, after 15 years, on November 29, 1999, my parole date finally arrived. My sister came to the prison to be with me and at 3:30p.m. we walked into the office of the parole board. Unlike what you might have seen on television where there is a group of people waiting, there was only one man that came in between myself and freedom. He was an older man and had one of those poker faces. There was no way that I could tell by the look on his face as to which way he would go. As I sat in front of him I was so nervous I could feel my knees shaking. I tried to keep them still but my mind simply wouldn't allow it. When I reached out to shake the man's hand my palms were wet with sweat.

Then he began: He asked me what happend that had caused me to come to prison. I explained that a man had hit my sister and in the process of protecting her we got into it and I ended up shooting the guy. I told him if I could take that day back I would. I would have handled the situation differently.

I went on to say that I was really sorry for my actions and sorry to his family and friends. He asked about the drug cases and I explained that I lived in the projects and due to having no father or proper guidance as well as being poor that I called myself making extra money to take care of my family.

He then asked about my assault ticket on staff in 1988, then about all the refusals to take urine tests. I explained, "I had sleepy eyes and I was always being accused of being high, when I'd never done drugs."

He then read my psychology report. At that point my

mind simply went blank because the report was pretty good, but that only caused more anxiety because I knew that after that report if I didn't get set free I may never go home. The report couldn't get much better. There was nothing negative about it. He finally asked if I had a job waiting if I was released and I told him yes.

Then he asked my sister did she have something to say. She stated that, my family needed me at home and that since our mother had passed that they were really in need of a man to take care of our family affairs. And just like that he told me that I had gotten my parole.

I couldn't believe it. Me and my sister both broke down crying.

It was a sad sight, but a happy occasion. It was the happiest day of my life. The counselor, Mr. Gleason got up and got us some napkins. He then asked if we were okay and then gave me some stern advice.

He told me not to go bragging about my parole because that would only cause other inmates to get jealous and even mad and try to make me loose it. He suggested that I tell them that I'd gotten a discussion for a parole which I was more than glad to do.

Well, I was put into a program to prepare me for the trip home. Yea those following months were hard. They even sent me to this nasty camp 100 miles away to spend my last days. It didn't make any sense to get sent that far away when I was already home but I was going home and I was not about to let anything get in the way of that. At this point, I didn't care how far they sent me. Just as long as they opened that door when my out date came.

It's been a few years now since I've been home. I wish my mother was around to see me doing well. It would have really made her proud to know that I've written a book, come out and gotten married and reacquainted myself with my child. But I know like any guardian angel she's looking down. She's given me the strength I need to stay positive, focused and optimistic about my life. Yes, freedom is a beautiful thing. Thank God for freedom.